D1569297

Where Credit Is Due

A Guide to Proper Citing of Sources—Print and Nonprint

Second Edition

Nancy E. Shields

with the assistance of Mary E. Uhle

The Scarecrow Press, Inc.
Lanham, Md., & London
1997

SCARECROW PRESS, INC.

Published in the United States of America
by Scarecrow Press, Inc.
4720 Boston Way
Lanham, Maryland 20706

4 Pleydell Gardens, Folkestone
Kent CT20 2DN, England

British Cataloguing-in-Publication Information Available

Library of Congress Cataloging-in-Publication Data

Shields, Nancy E.
    Where credit is due : a guide to proper citing of sources, print
and nonprint / Nancy E. Shields, Mary E. Uhle. — 2nd ed.
        p.   cm.
    Includes bibliographical references and index.
    ISBN 0-8108-3211-9 (cloth : alk. paper)
    1. Bibliographical citations.   2. Audio-visual materials—
Bibliography—Methodology.   I. Uhle, Mary E.   II. Title.
PN171.F56S35   1997
808'.027—dc21   96-6523
                                                     CIP

ISBN 0-8108-3211-9 (cloth: alk.paper)

Contents

Introduction

You, the student, are completing a research paper* or term paper,* which must include footnotes* and a bibliography.* How can you handle troublesome footnotes and bibliographic entries? Use this comprehensive, simplified, style guide.*

Why Use a Style Guide?

A style guide will help you properly document the sources you have used in your research/term paper. Correct documenting enables a reader to easily locate the source of your material for further information or verification. You must be careful to accurately credit a person for his or her own work. Taking the words or ideas of someone else and claiming them as your own is stealing; so, too, is failing to acknowledge the source of your material. The term for both of these is plagiarism.*

This guide does not include everything about footnotes and bibliographies—but probably includes more than you need to know! However, your task will be simplified if you follow the formats outlined here.

What sources can you use in a research/term paper? Everything! Not only all printed materials, but radio and TV programs, films, filmstrips, computer materials, videocassettes, speeches, lectures, audio recordings, microscope slides, works of art—these materials can be excellent references and should not be avoided simply because footnote and bibliographic information is hard to find.

This style guide provides examples of footnote and bibliographic entries for these sources and many others. Also included

---

*These terms are defined in the glossary.

1

are abbreviations, checklists, suggestions for completing your paper, sample pages, and clear definitions of terminology. The rest is up to you. Be careful, and good luck.

What Kinds of Printed Media* Can You Use for Research?

Almost any printed matter can be used; however, it is necessary to footnote—that is, acknowledge the source of—the material. Have you considered using these for your research?

_____ books (authored, edited, translated, compiled)

_____ encyclopedias (signed and unsigned articles)

_____ pamphlets*

_____ magazines (articles,* editorials,* columns,* reviews,* etc.)

_____ newspapers (articles, editorials, columns, reviews, etc.)

_____ literary works (poems, plays, etc.)

_____ Bible

_____ public or government documents*

_____ other reference books (almanacs, atlases, dictionaries, handbooks, manuals, yearbooks,* etc.)

_____ questionnaires*/surveys*

_____ flyers*/posters*/charts*

_____ speeches*/lectures*/sermons*

_____ interviews*

_____ dissertations*

_____ correspondence*

_____ unpublished material*

_____ Vertical file* material

*These terms are defined in the glossary.

_____ adaptations*

_____ fax* (facsimile) materials. (Note: Materials gathered by fax should be cited following the format of the original source, e.g., newspaper article, correspondence, survey.)

What Kinds of Nonprint Media* Can You Use for Research?

It's hard to imagine a nonprint source that can't be used. The only limit is the imagination! How imaginative have you been in your research?

_____ public speeches/lectures/sermons

_____ computer software*

_____ filmstrips

_____ media kits* (slides and records: filmstrips and cassettes, etc.)

_____ microscope slides*

_____ motion pictures/video recordings* (TV, videocassettes, etc.)

_____ photographs

_____ photographic slides

_____ audio recordings* (records, tapes, CDs,* etc.)

_____ transparencies*

_____ interviews

_____ radio broadcasts

_____ realia* (primitive tools, rock specimens, clothing, etc.)

_____ creative works* (museum pieces, musical compositions, blueprints, etc.)

*These terms are defined in the glossary.

_____   microforms* (microfilms, microfiche)

_____   telephone calls

_____   live performances (concerts, plays, ballet)

_____   interactive media,* interactive video,* computer/video

*What Information Do You Need for Footnote/Bibliographic Entries
for Print Media?*

The information varies and depends upon which print media you
are using.

Information Needed for BOOKS:

When using a book, get footnote/bibliographic information from
the title page and verso*—not from the cover or spine* of the
book. Some of this information may not be available.

_____   author(s), editor(s), compiler(s),* translator(s)*
            institution(s)

_____   name of book, including subtitle*

_____   publisher/publishing company

_____   copyright/publication date

_____   place of publication (If the city is not well known or
            could be confused with another city, include the state
            or country.)

_____   page number(s)

_____   volume number(s)/letter(s), if a multivolume set
            (for example, encyclopedia)

_____   title of article

_____   name and author of original work, if an adaptation

*These terms are defined in the glossary.

Information Needed for MAGAZINES and NEWSPAPERS:

When using a magazine or newspaper, get footnote/bibliographic information from the specific article, the table of contents page, or the editorial page. Some of this information may not be available.

_____ author(s), editor(s), reviewer(s), columnist(s)

_____ title/headline, including subtitle

_____ name of magazine/newspaper

_____ volume number

_____ date of publication

_____ place of publication (If the city is not well known or could be confused with another city, include state or country.)

_____ page number(s)

_____ section

_____ title of specific work being reviewed

_____ author of material being reviewed

Information Needed for OTHER PRINTED MEDIA:

When using other printed media, footnote/bibliographic information can be found in many places, such as title page, verso, back page, corner, inside front cover. Some of this information may not be available.

_____ author(s), editor(s), compiler(s), translator(s), institution(s)

_____ name of material, including subtitle

_____ publisher/publishing company/issuing department

_____ series name and number

_____ copyright/publication/issuing date

_____ place of publication (If the city is not well known or could be confused with another city, include state or country.)

_____ page number(s)

_____ location in a literary work (for example, stanza, line, scene, or act in poem or play)

_____ name and author of original work, if an adaptation

_____ format*

What Information Do You Need for Footnote/Bibliographic Entries for Nonprint Media?

When using nonprint media, footnote/bibliographic information can be found in many places, such as introductory/concluding frames, container/box, accompanying documentation, or the item itself. Some of this information may not be available.

_____ title of item, program, subject matter, etc.

_____ name of set or series

_____ format (for example, slide, record, videotape, film, cassette tape, computer software)

_____ author(s), director(s), program writer(s), producer(s), manufacturer(s), photographer(s), collector(s)

_____ artist(s)/performer(s)

_____ reader(s)/narrator(s)*/commentator(s),* broadcaster(s), instructor(s)

_____ identification number (for example, record number, cassette number)

_____ release/production/manufacture/broadcast/ performance/lecture date

_____ name and author of original work, if an adaptation

*These terms are defined in the glossary.

What Must You Do Before Starting Footnote/Bibliographic Entries?

You must have completed the following steps:

_____ chosen your subject;

_____ prepared your working bibliography*;

_____ limited or expanded your original subject, if necessary;

_____ prepared your working outline*;

_____ taken your notes;

_____ finalized your outline; and

_____ written your working draft.*

*These terms are defined in the glossary.

Footnotes

What is a footnote?

A footnote is your acknowledgment of the source of material, a comment on material, or an explanatory note about material.

When Do You Use a Footnote?

A footnote must be used for

1. a direct quote
2. a paraphrase* of an idea
3. a comment giving additional information
4. an explanatory statement or definition
5. a reference to another part of your paper

1. A Footnote Must Be Used for a Direct Quote.

Probably the best-known use of footnotes is for directly quoting, i.e., using someone else's exact words.

Exact quotation   "Commerce and industry have learned the power of color; girls in a factory complained of cold when the temperature was at 72 degrees, but the com-

---

*These terms are defined in the glossary.

plaints ceased when the blue-green
walls were painted coral; men lifting
black metal boxes complained of
strained backs, but when the same
boxes were painted pale green, said
that the new, light-weight boxes made a
real difference; . . ."[3]

Footnote   3. Ray Faulkner, Edwin Ziegfeld, and
Gerald Hill, *Art Today* (New York:
Henry Holt, 1949), 199.

2.   *A Footnote Must Be Used for a Paraphrase of an Idea.*

Even if you don't quote the words directly but paraphrase an
idea that is different and NOT common knowledge, you must
give credit to the author in a footnote. Common knowledge
is knowledge that is general, ordinary, widespread, or found in
dictionaries.

Your paraphrase   People working in factories stopped
complaining about the cold when
the blue-green walls were painted
coral, and men stopped complaining
about the weight of boxes when the
boxes were light green instead of
black.[4]

Footnote   4. Ray Faulkner, Edwin Ziegfeld, and
Gerald Hill, *Art Today* (New York:
Henry Holt, 1949), 199.

3.   *A Footnote Must Be Used for a Comment Giving
Additional Information.*

Sometimes you have additional information that you think might
interest or enlighten your reader; however, you don't really want to
include it in the text of your paper because it might distract, con-

fuse, or bore your reader. A footnote provides a good solution. The information is available for anyone who wants to read it, but it won't interrupt the flow of the main text of your paper.

Wording from text	The newly rich who were upwardly mobile and socially inclined longed to join the Four Hundred.[1]
Footnote	1. The Four Hundred took their name from the statements of a 19th century writer who claimed there were only about 400 people in New York City society who were at ease in a ballroom.

4. *A Footnote Must Be Used for an Explanatory Statement or Definition.*

There will be times when you find it necessary to explain a statement or define a term used in the text. To avoid interrupting the flow of your material, a footnote should be used.

Wording from text	Seeing James's name on the masthead[2] made his mother very proud.
Footnote	2. Masthead—a statement of the name, ownership, etc., of a publication. It is usually found at the head of the editorial page of a newspaper. In a magazine, it is usually on the editorial or contents page.

5. *A Footnote Must Be Used for a Reference to Another Part of Your Paper.*

If you have included an appendix,* glossary,* etc., you may want to direct your reader to that part of the paper by use of a footnote.

*These terms are defined in the glossary.

Wording from text	It is possible to grow a wide variety of crops in Ghana because of the climate and ample rainfall.[5]
Footnote	5. Graph showing average rainfall in Ghana is included in the Appendix.

Warning

Use of material other than your own may be dangerous unless you properly acknowledge its source. Failure to do so may result in charges of PLAGIARISM.

How Do You Number Footnotes?

Footnotes are numbered consecutively, and the number is normal in size, followed by a period and space. In the text the number always comes at the end of the material being noted and is raised above the line. In the footnote the number comes at the beginning of the notation.

Note: Traditionally, both the footnote number in the text and at the beginning of the footnote were raised above the line; however modern footnoting style uses raised numbers *only* in the text.

Direct quote in text	"So beautiful were the Mohawk's contours that the sight was miraculous."[6]
Footnote	6. Mary U. Hamilton, *The Magnificent Mohawk* (NY: Channel Press, 1993), 70.
Author's name in text	. . . as Michael[7] observed in his study . . .
Footnote	7. Jordan Michael, *The Story of Humanity* (Manshe, ID: Peoples & Liveright, 1971), 6.

Paraphrase   Like our educational system, good
in text   libraries, or the lack of them, affect every
                  American; and with the newer curricu-
                  lum methods, which are putting more
                  and more emphasis on research and
                  library-oriented skills, success or failure
                  educationally, socially, economically,
                  and culturally will be greatly determined
                  by the policies and services of our public
                  libraries and the response of individuals
                  to their library and its programs.[8]

Footnote   8. Erin A. Thomas, *Library Vitality*
                  (New Amsterdam, NY: Nantom
                  Medias, 1979), 441.

NOTE: In the text there is no space between the footnote
        number and the word or punctuation mark it
        follows.

EXAMPLE:

. . . to eliminate Plato."[9]

NOT

. . . to eliminate Plato." [9]

In the footnote notation, the number is normal size,
followed by a period and a space.

EXAMPLE:

   10. Richard Josephs, *Medieval Castles* (Geneseo, NY:
Social Times Press, 1984), 345.

NOT

[10]Richard Josephs, *Medieval Castles* (Geneseo, NY: Social
Times Press, 1984), 345.

**Do You Have to Rewrite the Full Footnote Every Time
a Source is Used?**

No. The first notation for a source must be written out completely
using the appropriate form; however, second and subsequent references are a different story. You can use the more traditional
abbreviations, such as, ibid.*, op. cit.*, and loc. cit.*; or you can use
the modern notation, which is a shortened version of the original
footnote; or you can give the notation in the text.

Ask your instructor which form is preferred. Whichever form
you use, be consistent throughout your paper.

1.   *Traditional Notation Uses the Abbreviations Ibid., Op. Cit., and
     Loc. Cit. for Second and Subsequent References to the Same Source.*

Ibid. is used when references to the same source are CONSECU-
TIVE, whether the page number(s) are the same or not.

EXAMPLE:

Original footnote   5. Benjamin Caruthers, *The History of
                       New Bedford* (Springfield, MA: Ahab &
                       Son, 1990), 87.

Abbreviated   6. Ibid., 202–4.
form: same
work, different
page

Abbreviated   7. Ibid.
form: same
work, same
page

Op. cit. is used when references to the same source are NOT
CONSECUTIVE and refer to DIFFERENT page number(s).

EXAMPLE:

Original footnote   2. Seaman Rivers, *Why Whaling?*
                       (Boston: Melville Books, 1899), 63.

*These terms are defined in the glossary.

Intervening *footnote*	3. Isaiah Bingham, *Women of New England* (Boston: Peabody Press, 1985), 111–5.
Abbreviated form	7. Rivers, op. cit., 22.
Abbreviated form	9. Bingham, op. cit., 21.

Loc. cit. is used when references to the same source are NOT CONSECUTIVE but refer to the SAME page number(s).

EXAMPLE:

Original footnote	10. Ishmael Waters, *Moby and Friends* (New York: Harpoon Press, 1888), 419.
Intervening footnote	11. Dick Herman, *Massachusetts Memoirs* (Cambridge: Crimson Press, 1902), 16.
Abbreviated form	12. Waters, loc. cit.

NOTE: Most authorities consider these abbreviations anglicized; therefore, ibid., op. cit., and loc. cit. do not need to be underlined or italicized.

2. *The Modern Notation Uses a Shortened Version for Second and Subsequent References to the Same Source.*

Remember, the *first* time you footnote a source, the full citation must be used. The form for the shortened version does not vary with a change in page number.

EXAMPLE:

Original footnote	1. Benjamin Caruthers, *The History of New Bedford* (Springfield, MA: Ahab & Son, 1990), 87.

Shortened   2. Caruthers, 102.
version

If you have more than one author with the same last name, use the first name or initial so your reader will not be confused.

EXAMPLE:

3. M. White, 21.

OR

3. Margaret White, 21.

If you use two books by the same author, you should include either the full title or an abbreviated form so your reader will know which book is indicated.

EXAMPLE:

4. Martin, *Fountain of Mercy*, 50.

OR

4. Martin, *Fountain*, 50.

5. Martin, *Barry's Lamp: A Gift Most Cherished*, 500.

OR

5. Martin, *Barry's*, 500.

Are There Shortened Terms That Can Be Used in Footnotes?

Yes, the modern form allows for the modification of the more traditional methods of notation. These changes include:

1. use of the ampersand (&) in the publisher's name

EXAMPLE:

Thatcher and Sons

NOW

Thatcher & Sons

> When using any of these shortened forms, be consistent throughout the paper.

2. deletion of terms such as "Company," "Inc.," "Ltd.," "Corp.," and "S.A." in the publisher's name

EXAMPLE:

Jardin Company

NOW

Jardin

Research Models, Inc.

NOW

Research Models

3. deletion of "The" in the publisher's name

EXAMPLE:

The Current Press

NOW

Current Press

> When using any of these shortened forms, be consistent throughout the paper.

4. use of state and country abbreviations in place of publication

EXAMPLE:

Colorado	England
NOW	NOW
CO	Eng.

NOTE: Do not abbreviate New York when referring to the city. However, when referring to the state, use NY.

If you are not familiar with the recommended abbreviations for states and countries, see abbreviations section in the Appendix.

5. deletion of p. and pp. in page number references.

EXAMPLE:

pp. 112–115

NOW

112–115

6. deletion of numerals in page numbers

EXAMPLE:

112–115

NOW

112–5

7. use of the abbreviation for line/lines

EXAMPLE:

line 14

NOW

l. 14

lines 26–43

NOW

ll. 26–43

8. use of the abbreviation for stanza in poetry

EXAMPLE:

stanza 3

NOW

st. 3

When using any of these shortened forms, be consistent throughout the paper.

What Do Sample Footnotes Look Like in Traditional Notation?

1. Benjamin Caruthers, *The History of New Bedford* (Springfield, Massachusetts: Ahab and Son, 1990), p. 87.
2. Ibid., p. 89.
3. Seaman Rivers, *Why Whaling?* (Boston: Melville Books, 1899), p. 63.
4. Ibid.
5. Ibid.
6. Isaiah Bingham, *Women of New England* (Boston: Peabody Press, 1985), pp. 111–115.
7. Caruthers, op. cit., p. 79.
8. Bingham, loc. cit.
9. Ishmael Waters, *Moby and Friends* (New York: Harpoon Press, 1888), p. 419.
10. Rivers, op. cit., p. 81.
11. Caruthers, loc. cit.
12. Dick Herman, *Massachusetts Memoirs* (Cambridge, MA: Crimson Press, 1902), p. 16.
13. Ibid., p. 20.
14. Waters, op. cit., p. 424.
15. Ibid.

NOTE: The shortened version seems to be used more frequently than this traditional method.

What Do Sample Footnotes Look Like in Modern Notation?

1. Benjamin Caruthers, *The History of New Bedford* (Springfield, MA: Ahab & Son, 1990), 87.
2. Caruthers, 89.
3. Seaman Rivers, *Why Whaling?* (Boston: Melville Books, 1899), 63.
4. Rivers, 63.
5. Rivers, 63.
6. Isaiah Bingham, *Women of New England* (Boston: Peabody Press, 1985), 111–5.
7. Caruthers, 79.
8. Bingham, 111–5.
9. Ishmael Waters, *Moby and Friends* (New York: Harpoon Press, 1888), 419.
10. Rivers, 81.
11. Caruthers, 79.
12. Dick Herman, *Massachusetts Memoirs* (Cambridge, MA: Crimson Press, 1902), 16.
13. Herman, 20.
14. Waters, 424.
15. Waters, 424.

NOTE: Check with your instructor as to which method of notation is preferred.

Can You Use Information Already Footnoted, i.e., Secondary Source* Material?

Yes. Your footnote citation must show the source YOU are using as well as the ORIGINAL footnote, i.e., the footnote cited in the work you are using. However, your bibliographic citation shows only the source you are using. For sample citations, see Secondary Source Material in the footnote and bibliography sections.

Where Do You Put Footnotes in a Research/Term Paper?

Footnotes can be put in different places—usually at the bottom of each page or at the end of the research/term paper; however, the APA* style includes the source within the text.

*These terms are defined in the glossary.

If you put footnotes at the bottom of the page, each footnote must be on the same page of text as its corresponding footnote number. If you put footnotes at the back of the paper, they must be on a separate page(s) with the centered heading "Notes" on the first page only. For samples of this way of entering footnotes see sample pages in the Appendix.

Remember, no matter where you place footnotes, they are numbered consecutively. (APA does not use numbers. See sample in Appendix.)

> NOTE: If you can choose where to put footnotes, you will find it easier to type them in a separate section at the end of the paper.

Footnoting Printed Materials

How Do You Write a Footnote Entry for a Book?

This is a general guide for footnoting a BOOK; however, THERE ARE MANY DIFFERENCES. Make sure you follow the specific examples. For ADAPTATIONS, see citations under Adaptation.

Reference books such as dictionaries, atlases, almanacs, manuals, and handbooks follow the sample in the box. Specific examples of the most commonly used reference books are also included.

---

1. author's name, *title of book* (place of publication: publisher, date of publication), page #.

> NOTE: The information necessary for a book citation can be found on the title page and/or verso.

Book with one author
> 1. Sam Johnson, *The Memoirs of Frannie Lapp* (Houston: Monkey Press, 1989), 28.

Book with two authors
> 2. Marvin Tishner and Bernard Schwartz, *Colored Prism: Hues of Green* (New York: Large Press, 1988), 50.

NOTE: "Hues of Green" is a subtitle, separated from the title by a colon.

Book with three authors	3. Ray Oates, Edwin Barley, and Gerald Rye, *Wheat for the World* (San Diego: Clyde Colt & Sons, 1991), 199.
Book with more than three authors	4. Nia Ashbridge and others, *Tracing Your English Ancestors* (New York: Blackcourt, 1990), 121–5.

OR

4. Nia Ashbridge, et al., *Tracing Your English Ancestors* (New York: Blackcourt, 1990), 121–5.

Book with association/ institution as author	5. American Media Association, *Guide to Media Centers* (Chicago: American Media Association, 1988), 101.
Book with no author	6. *Images on the Water* (Seaton, MS: D. Pierce, 1980), 17.
Book with editor and author	7. Richard Erwin Moose, *The History of Livingston County*, ed. by Edward M. Cox (Rochester, NY: Genesee Press, 1987), 419.
Book with editor and no author	8. Judy Pine, ed., *Great Trees of North America* (Dallas: Greenleaf & Trunk, 1992), 15.
Book with compiler and no author	9. Geraldine Reynard, comp., *Thrift Shops in New England* (Springtown, NH: Penrose, 1990), 88.
Book with author and translator	10. Everett Chips, *Troubleshooting Computers,* trans. by Erin DeLuca (Danbury, CT: Hatter Press, 1994), 42.

Book with translator and no author	11. Edward D. Gundermodd, trans., *Treatises from the Roman Courts* (Rome: Italian Press, 1987), 60.
Dictionary	12. E. L. Thornton, ed., *Thornton Dictionary*, 4th ed. (Peoria, IL: Johnson Southerby, 1994), 877.
Atlas	13. *Great World Atlas*, 5th ed. (Wappingers Falls, NY: Hopewell Press, 1995), 130.
Almanac	14. "Education: New Jersey." *Reader's 1995 Almanac* (Paterson, NJ: Trenton Releases, 1995), 227.

How Do You Write a Footnote Entry for a Pamphlet?

This is a general guide for footnoting a PAMPHLET; however, THERE ARE MANY DIFFERENCES. Make sure you follow the specific examples.

---

1. author's name, *title of pamphlet* (place of publication: publisher, date of publication), page #.

NOTE: The information necessary for a pamphlet citation can be found on the front cover, title page, verso, inside back cover, back cover, and/or last page of the pamphlet. Some of the information may not be available.

Pamphlet with author	1. Paul Housing, *Revitalizing the Inner City* (Detroit: Committee for Social Improvement, 1992), 10.
Pamphlet with no author	2. *Plague* (Washington: U.S. Government Printing Office, 1989), 5.

Pamphlet with an association/ institution as author	3. Committee on Fair Labor Practices, *The Effect of Bankruptcy on Negotiating a Union Contract* (Washington: American Federation of Union Breakers, 1994), 13.

How Do You Write a Footnote Entry for an Encyclopedia Article?

This is a general guide for footnoting an ENCYCLOPEDIA ARTI-CLE; however, THERE ARE MANY DIFFERENCES. Make sure you follow the specific examples.

---

1. article author's name, "title of article," *name of encyclopedia* (date of publication), volume number/letter, page #.

NOTE: The information necessary for an encyclopedia article citation can be found on the title page, verso of the specific volume used (or of the first volume of the set or of the index volume), and/or on the article itself.

Signed encyclopedia article	1. William J. Brown, "Twentieth Century Architecture," *Encyclopedia Americana* (1991), XXVI, 147–55.
Unsigned encyclopedia article	2. "Dogs," *Encyclopaedia Britannica* (1994), IV, 85.
Signed encyclopedia article in yearbook	3. Guy Greene, "Hot Air Balloons," *The 1992 World Book Year Book* (1992), 77.
Unsigned encyclopedia article in one-volume encyclopedia	4. "Computers," *Columbia Encyclopedia,* 5th ed. (1990), 80.

How Do You Write a Footnote Entry for a Magazine Article?

This is a general guide for footnoting a MAGAZINE ARTICLE; however, THERE ARE MANY DIFFERENCES. Make sure you follow the specific examples.

---

1. article author's name, "title of article," *name of magazine,* date of *magazine,* page #.

NOTE: The information necessary for a magazine article citation can be found on the table of contents page, editorial page, and/or on the specific article being used.

Signed article 1. B. Grumet, "The Law and the Battered Child," *PTA Magazine,* December 1990, 133–6.

Unsigned article 2. "Caps for Christmas," *The Bottle Capper* (IA), October 1983, 16.

NOTE: If the magazine is not generally known, the state is put in parentheses following the name of the magazine.

Signed review 3. Herbert Boone, "There Is Fairness,"
with title rev. of *Discrimination* (Genesee Press) by William Whimper in *Sports Illustrated,* February 17, 1992, 88.

NOTE: Following the title of the review, indicate the name of the work being reviewed, its publisher/producer, and/or its author.

Signed review 4. Martha Holbine, rev. of "Primary
with no title Spotlight" (NBC), in *The Maine Sun,* August 17, 1994, 6.

Editorial with title	5. "Jimmy Jock," Editorial, *Sport*, August 17, 1993, 29.
Editorial with no title	6. Editorial, *Mademoiselle*, April 1991, 6.

NOTE: Since most editorials are unsigned, the footnote begins with the editorial title, if given. If no title is indicated, begin the footnote with the word "Editorial."

Signed column with title	7. Bill Ways, "Ramblings," Column, *Travel Lore*, May 8, 1994, 12.
Signed column with no title	8. Mike Fine, Column, *World of Stereo*, July 1993, 4.

How Do You Write a Footnote Entry for a Newspaper Article?

This is a general guide for footnoting a NEWSPAPER ARTICLE; however, THERE ARE MANY DIFFERENCES. Make sure you follow the specific examples.

---

1. article author's name, "title/headline of article," *name of newspaper*, date of newspaper, section #, page #.

NOTE: The information necessary for a newspaper article citation can be found on the table of contents page, editorial page, and/or on the specific article being used.

Signed article   1. Joseph Ambrose, "Riot Erupts in Capital City," *Boonetown Standard* (TN), December 1, 1991, Section I, 8.

NOTE: If the newspaper is not generally known, the state is put in parentheses following the name of the newspaper.

Unsigned article	2. "Pilgrims Flock to Jerusalem," *The Jerusalem Post,* June 22, 1994, 1.
Signed review with title	3. Joseph Edwards, "The Wee Asp," rev. of "Gidget Goes Boston" (Bombast Films) in *The New England Weekly,* March 21, 1965, 12.

NOTE: Following the title of the review indicate the name of the work being reviewed, its publisher/producer and/or author.

Signed review with no title	4. Cora Critic, rev. of *Modern Shakespeare* (Billboard Press) by Richard Old, in New Republic, March 21, 1993, 16–18.
Editorial with title	5. "Where's the Water?" Editorial, *Arizona Pioneer,* July 3, 1990, 9.
Editorial with no title	6. Editorial, *London Messenger,* May 25, 1993, Section II, 25.

NOTE: Since most editorials are unsigned, the footnote begins with the editorial title, if given. If no title is indicated, begin the footnote with the word "Editorial."

Signed column with title	7. Mary Kohan, "As I Was Saying . . .," Column, *Bronx Review,* September 11, 1992, 16.
Signed column with no title	8. Marlene Martyr, Column, *Sioux City Press,* August 25, 1994, 15.

How Do You Write a Footnote Entry for a Poem?

This is a general guide for footnoting a POEM; however, THERE ARE MANY DIFFERENCES. Make sure you follow the specific examples. For ADAPTATIONS, see citations under Adaptation.

> 1. author's name, "title of poem," stanza # and/or line(s)
> (place of publication: publisher, date of publication), page #.

NOTE: The information necessary for a poetic citation can be found on the title page, verso, table of contents page, editorial page, and/or on the poem itself.

Single poem	1. Robert Billowy, "Ode to the Spanish Sails," st. 3, l. 16–21 (San Jose, CA: Nautical Press, 1980).

NOTE: In some cases the lines/stanzas of a poem may not be numbered. If necessary for the purpose of identification, lines/stanzas should be counted and noted in poetic citations.

Anonymous poem	2. "Night of the Knight," st. 1–4, ll. 1–24 (Camelot, Eng.: Stillwell & Sons, 1985).
Poem in an anthology/ collection by author	3. Scotty MacKeel, "Loch Ness Me," st. 2 quoted in *Scotland's Heritage* (Lansing, MI: Edinboro Publications, 1991), 93.
Poem in an anthology/ collection with an editor	4. Susan J. Dewy, "Ballad of the Rain," ll. 8–12 quoted by Thomas Weatherbee, ed., in *Rainbow Lyrics* (Sun City, FL: Solar & Sons, 1990), 37.
Poem in an anthology/ collection with a compiler	5. Angelo Deisel, "People of Germany," st. 1, ll. 4–8 quoted by Charles Vaughan, comp., in *Poems of the World* (Pontiac, NV: Kutchman & Son, 1986), 21.
Poem in a periodical	6. Monica Von Pelt, "Warm Fuzzies," st. 4 quoted in *Furtrappers' Monthly* (SD), December 1988, 11.

How Do You Write a Footnote Entry for a Play?

This is a general guide for footnoting a PLAY; however, THERE ARE MANY DIFFERENCES. Make sure you use the specific examples. For ADAPTATIONS, see citations under Adaptation.

---

1. author's name, *title of play*, act # and/or scene #, line(s) (place of publication: publisher, date of publication), page #.

NOTE: The information necessary for a play citation can be found on the title page, verso, table of contents page, editorial page, and/or on the play itself.

Single play   1. William Handsome, *The Raising of My Father*, I, i (Padre, NM: Pops Press, 1990).

NOTE: Standard roman numeral notation is used to indicate act (upper case) and scene (lower case) in play citations.

Anonymous play   2. *Seagulls on the Waterfront*, III, iv, ll. 1–27 (Bayonne, NJ: Bird-Sky Prints, 1991).

NOTE: In some cases the lines of a play may not be numbered. If necessary for the purpose of identification, lines should be counted and noted in play citations.

One-act play   3. Jeannette Matson, *Truth*, one act, ll. 69–84 (Honesty, WV: Purity Publications, 1993).

Play in an   4. Linda Cammarosano, *Our Cam-*
anthology/   *paigningHorizon*, V, iii, ll. 101–32
collection   quoted in *On the Political Side of Life*
by author   (Albany, NY: Tom Sander Associates, 1994), 65–6.

Play in an anthology/ collection with an editor	5. Wenda Wordsmith, *One Sparkling Moment,* II, ii, l. 15 quoted by I. Penworth, ed., in *Plays for a Romantic Evening* (San Diego: Dramatic Press, 1989), 123.
Play in an anthology/ collection with a compiler	6. George Floral, *Tulip Time,* I, i, ll. 15–35 quoted by Rose Arbor, comp., in *Blossoming Freedoms* (Garden City, NY: Horticultural Press, 1992), 23–4.
Play in a periodical	7. Libby Breakage, *Keys of Glass,* III, iii, ll. 54–63 quoted in *Interpretive Plays,* September 1992, 12–3.

How Do You Write a Footnote Entry for a Short Story?

This is a general guide for footnoting a SHORT STORY; however, THERE ARE MANY DIFFERENCES. Make sure you follow the specific examples. For ADAPTATIONS, see citations under Adaptation.

---

1. author's name, "title of short story" (place of publication: publisher, date of publication), page #.

NOTE: The information necessary for a short story citation can be found on the title page, verso, table of contents page, editorial page, and/or on the story itself.

Single short story	1. Scarlet Blaque, "Artist's Palette" (Red Hook, MT: Crimson Press, 1988), 4.
Short story in anthology/ collection by author	2. Etan Browne, "Blew Prism" quoted in *Kaleidoscope Memories* (Orange Oaks, NJ: Hue & Son, 1994), 55–6.

Short story in anthology/ collection with an editor	3. Terra Blanc, "Ebony" quoted by Herbert Canarie, ed., in *Verde's Mountain* (Black Hills, ND: Yelo-Press Publications, 1991), 121.
Short story in anthology/ collection with a compiler	4. Elicia Rouge, "Lilac Nights" quoted by Frances Whyte, comp., in *Horizons Forever* (Denville, TX: Rainbow Press, 1990), 20–8.
Short story in a periodical	5. Grey Fields, "Mother's Colorful Childhood" quoted in *The Artists' Family Journal* (RI), June 1991, 13.

How Do You Write a Footnote Entry for an Essay?

This is a general guide for footnoting an ESSAY; however, THERE ARE MANY DIFFERENCES. Make sure you follow the specific examples. For ADAPTATIONS, see citations under Adaptation.

---

1. author's name, "title of essay" (place of publication: publisher, date of publication), page #.

NOTE:	The information necessary for an essay citation can be found on the title page, verso, table of contents page, editorial page, and/or on the essay itself.

Single essay	1. Allegro McKiernan, "Soothing Sounds" (Nyack, NY: Andante Composers, 1993), 2.
Anonymous essay	2. "Brother Is Ever-Present" (Wichita, KS: All Eyes Press, 1994), 3.
Essay in an anthology/ collection by author	3. Hamilton Frank, "Colonial Rights" quoted in *Revolutionary Times* (Philadelphia: Underdog Publications, 1970), 8.

Essay in an anthology/ collection with an editor	4. Stanley Cice, "Always Alibi-ing" quoted by Robbyn Hallett, ed., in *Excuses Anonymous* (Brewster, MA: My-Time Press, 1989), 4.
Essay in an anthology/ collection with a compiler	5. Ernestine Elh, "Germanic Arts" quoted by Evelyn Anders, comp., in *European Art Treasures* (Florence, IT: Franco & Franco, 1991), 31.
Essay in a periodical	6. Sylvian Samuels, "Nature's Bounty" quoted in *Eastern Evergreen* (NH), October 1990, 11–2.

How Do You Write a Footnote Entry for the Transcript of a Speech, Lecture, or Sermon?

This is a general guide for footnoting a printed SPEECH, LECTURE, or SERMON; however, THERE ARE MANY DIFFERENCES. Make sure you use the specific examples. For ADAPTATIONS, see citations under Adaptation. The form below is for a PRINTED speech, lecture, or sermon; for a NONPRINT speech, lecture, or sermon, see citations in the nonprint section.

The transcript of a speech, lecture, or sermon is defined as a written message given to an individual or audience for a specific purpose.

---

1. speaker's name, identification of speaker, "title of speech/lecture/sermon" (place of publication: publisher, date of publication), page # [format].

NOTE: The information necessary for a printed speech, lecture, or sermon citation can be found on the title page, verso, table of contents page, editorial page, and/or on the speech/lecture/sermon itself.

Single speech/ lecture/sermon	1. B.A. Bradley, Pastor of Stone Heights Chapel, "Religious

Resurrection" (El, Ger.: Annunciation Publications, 1985), 3 [sermon].

Anonymous speech/lecture/sermon

2. "On Wings of Angels" (Saulte Saint Marie, MI: Archangel Publications, December 25, 1991), 2 [sermon].

Speech/lecture/sermon in anthology/collection by author

3. Reymon Pulse, M.D., Chief of Medical Services at Getwel Hospital, "Effects of Nuclear Radiation on Brain Cells" quoted in *Pulse's Essays on Nuclear Medicine* (Grosse Point, MI: Medical Arts, 1983), 67–70 [lecture].

Speech/lecture/sermon in anthology/collection with an editor

4. Pamela Mith, Curator of Medieval Museum, "Unicorns: Fact or Fiction?" quoted by Bobbi Ballad, ed., in *Animals in Legend* (Whitehorse, MT: Fantasy Fiction, 1993), 6–16 [speech].

Speech/lecture/sermon in anthology/collection with a compiler

5. Elsie Shampoo, Cosmetology Instructor at Technical Trades, "Cutting Techniques" quoted by Nancy Browne, comp., in *Modern Hair* (Los Angeles: Cosmo Paperbacks, 1992), 7 [lecture].

Speech/lecture/sermon in a periodical

6. William Summ, Economist, "The Wall Street Bulls and Bears" quoted in *American Pauper* (New York), July 17, 1985, 41 [speech].

How Do You Write a Footnote Entry for the Transcript of a Conference, Convention, or Seminar?

This is a general guide for footnoting the transcript of a CONFERENCE, CONVENTION, or SEMINAR. For a live or video conference, convention, or seminar, see citations in the nonprint section.

The transcript of a conference, convention, or seminar is defined as the written record of such proceedings.

---

1. sponsoring organization's name, "title of conference convention/seminar" (place of publication: publisher, date of publication), page # [format].

NOTE: The information necessary for conference, conven-
        tion, or seminar proceedings citation can usually
        be found on the title page, verso, and/or table of
        contents page.

Conference/   1. American Association of Cable
convention/   Networks, "Vision for the 21st
seminar   Century" (Atlanta: American
proceedings   Association of Cable Networks,
                     September 1994), 50 [convention].

How Do You Write a Footnote Entry for the Transcript of an Interview?

This is a general guide for footnoting a printed INTERVIEW; however, THERE ARE MANY DIFFERENCES. Make sure you follow
the specific examples. The form below is for a PRINTED interview;
for a NONPRINT interview, see citations in the nonprint section.

---

1. interviewee's name, identification of interviewee, interviewed by interviewer's name, "title/subject of interview,"
date of interview, quoted by compiler's/editor's name,
comp./ed., in *title of book/periodical* (place of publication:
publisher, date of publication), page #.

NOTE: The information necessary for an interview citation
        can be found on the title page, verso, table of con-
        tents page, editorial page, and/or on the interview
        itself.

Interview in an   1. Sally Starlet, Actress, interviewed by
anthology/   Sue Leffler, "Stardom Is Not Roses,"

collection with an editor	February 23, 1990, quoted by Virginia N. Starr, ed., in *Meet the Celebrities* (Media, PA: Thalberg Publishing, 1991), 63.
Interview in an anthology/ collection with a compiler	2. H. Harold Homberg, U.N. Delegate from Great Britain, interviewed by Martin Kope, "H. Harold Homberg," November 11, 1991, quoted by Jon X. Mather, comp., in *Contemporary Statesmen* (New York: Plaza Publications, 1993), 2–3.
Interview in a periodical	3. Jacques Doubleday, Olympic Medalist, interviewed by Mahre Caruthers, "Living Skis," January 27, 1993, quoted in *Sporting Monthly*, February 1993, 21–3.

NOTE: If an interview is untitled, provide your own title based on the subject.

How Do You Write a Footnote Entry for a Biblical Reference?

This is a general guide for footnoting a BIBLICAL REFERENCE. Make sure you follow the specific examples.

---

1. book no. name of book chapter: verse(s).

NOTE: The information necessary for a biblical citation can be found on the beginning page of the specific book being used (for book number and name), on the top of the page containing the material (for chapter), and before the specific verse(s).

Numbered book	1. I Kings 9:5–8.
Unnumbered book	2. Mark 9:23.

How Do You Write a Footnote Entry for a Document, Questionnaire, or Survey?

This is a general guide for footnoting a DOCUMENT, QUESTIONNAIRE, or SURVEY; however, THERE ARE MANY DIFFERENCES. Make sure you follow the specific examples.

---

1. issuing department/bureau/person, *title of document/ questionnaire/survey* (place of publication: publisher, issuing date), series name, series number, page # [format].

NOTE: The information necessary for a document/questionnaire/survey citation can be found on the cover, on the title page, in a corner, and/or on the back of the item itself.

Public document
1. Committee for Extension Education, *The Need for a Community College in Putnam County* (Alta, ME: Marist College, December 1993), 2 [public document].

Government document
2. Communicable Disease Center, *Widget's Syndrome* (Atlanta: U.S. Government Printing Office, 1992), Viral Disease Series, No. 15, 4–5 [government document].

Organization document
3. Brewster Teachers' Association Welfare Fund, *The Welfunder* (Brewster, NY: Brewster Teachers' Association Welfare Fund, January 1995), 2 [newsletter].

Questionnaire
4. Archin Memorial Library, *What Public Library Services Have You Used?* (n.p.: Archin Memorial Library, Summer 1989), 1 [questionnaire].

Survey   5. Rudolph Claus, *Additional Expenses Incurred During the Period Beginning November 25 and Ending December 25* (Sleigh, NY: Rudolph Claus, February 17, 1992), 3 [survey].

NOTE: Many times the issuing department/bureau/person is also the publisher; repeat the name if this is the case.

How Do You Write a Footnote Entry for a Congressional Record Reference?

This is a general guide for footnoting the *CONGRESSIONAL RECORD*. Make sure you follow the specific examples.

---

1. *Congressional Record*. date of legislative proceeding: page #.

NOTE: The information necessary for a *Congressional Record* citation can be found on the document itself.

Congressional   1. *Cong. Rec.* Aug. 16, 1994: 7550–71.
Record

How Do You Write a Footnote Entry for a Flyer, Poster, or Chart?

This is a general guide for footnoting a FLYER, POSTER, or CHART. Make sure you follow the specific examples.

---

1. issuing organization/person, *title/subject of flyer/poster/chart* (place of publication: publisher, issuing date) [format].

NOTE: The information necessary for a flyer, poster, or chart citation can usually be found on the back or in a corner of the item itself.

Flyer   1. Concerned Citizens of Mt. Morris, *School Consolidation: Yes or No* (n.p.:

Concerned Citizens of Mt. Morris, April 1989) [flyer].

NOTE: Sometimes the issuing organization/person is the same as the publisher; repeat the name if this is the case.

Poster   2. United Lobster Fishermen, *Ban Offshore Drilling* (Moosebay, ME: Moosebay Chamber of Commerce, 1990) [poster].

Chart   3. Melvil Dewey, *The Dewey Decimal Classification* (Amherst: Media Charts, 1987) [chart].

How Do You Write a Footnote Entry for a Dissertation?

This is a general guide for footnoting a DISSERTATION. Make sure you follow the specific examples.

---

1. author's name, "title of dissertation" (place of publication/issuance: publisher/issuing agent, date of publication/issuance), page # [format].

NOTE: The information necessary for a dissertation citation can be found on the document itself.

Published   1. Joseph A. McKiernan, "The
dissertation   Economic Impact of Computers on
                   Secondary Social Studies Education"
                   (New City, NY: Social Trends Press,
                   1993), 21. [published dissertation].

Unpublished   2. Julieanne Lawrence-Russell,
dissertation   "Testing Procedures for Placement in
                   Gifted and Talented Programs in
                   Elementary Schools" (Saratoga Springs,

NY: St. Luther Univ., 1991), 67 [unpub-
lished dissertation].

How Do You Write a Footnote Entry for Correspondence?

This is a general guide for footnoting CORRESPONDENCE.
Make sure you follow the specific examples.

---

1. author's name, identification of author, correspondence
to recipient's name (date of correspondence).

NOTE: The information necessary for a correspondence
citation can be found on the document itself. Some
of the information may not be available.

Personal correspondence	1. Henrietta Dearborne, correspondence to Erin Essex (March 20, 1994).
Business correspondence	2. James W. Asp, President of Tri-State Electronics, correspondence to Paula Cox (May 17, 1993).
Open correspondence	3. Congressman Samuel S. Statz, Maine representative 23rd District, correspondence to constituents (January 20, 1992).

How Do You Write a Footnote Entry for Unpublished Material?

This is a general guide for footnoting UNPUBLISHED MATER-
IAL; however, THERE ARE MANY DIFFERENCES. Make sure
you follow the specific examples.

Unpublished material is defined as printed matter that has
been released for *limited* distribution.

---

1. author's name, "title of unpublished material" (place of
issuance: issuing agent, date) [unpublished material].

NOTE: The information necessary for an unpublished
        material citation can be found on the document
        itself. Some of the information may not be available.

Information   1. Silver Spade Garden Club, "Spring
sheet   Gardening Guidelines." (Silver Spade
                       Garden Club, 1990) [unpublished
                       material].

NOTE: Many times the author is also the issuing agent;
        repeat the name if this is the case.

Employee notice   2. John Allan Mohler, "Some Issues of
                       Concern." (Bedford Heights, LA: Board
                       of Education, March 1993) [unpub-
                       lished material].

Classroom handout   3. "Causes of the Revolutionary War."
                     [unpublished material].

Church bulletin   4. Julia A. Bargelo, ed., "The Chimes."
                       (Weirton, WV: Sacred Heart on the Hill,
                       December 25, 1993) [unpublished
                       material].

How Do You Write a Footnote Entry for Material from a Vertical File?

This is a general guide for footnoting VERTICAL FILE MATE-
RIAL; however, THERE ARE MANY DIFFERENCES. Make sure
you follow the specific examples.

   If an item can be footnoted according to its particular category
(magazine or newspaper article, pamphlet, etc.) use the appropriate footnote documentation style. Sometimes the information necessary for these items is incomplete or missing, in which case the
vertical file format should be used.

---

   1. author's name, "title of specific item" (place of publication: publisher, date) [vertical file—format].

NOTE: The information necessary for a citation for vertical file material can usually be found on the item itself. Some of the information may not be available.

Map in   1. "Australia" (Sydney, Austral.: Koala
vertical file   Cartography, 1988) [vertical file—map].

Documentation   2. "Marines Take Iwo Jima" (*New York*
missing   *Times*) [vertical file—newspaper article].

NOTE: In this case the author, date, and page number are missing.

How Do You Write a Footnote Entry for Secondary Source Material?

This is a general guide for footnoting SECONDARY SOURCE MATERIAL; however, THERE ARE MANY DIFFERENCES. Make sure you follow the specific examples.

If the secondary source material you are using is not given here, use the basic form in the box and consult specific footnote examples in this book for the combination needed.

Secondary source material is defined as a reference to part(s) of an original work/writing or to a segment(s) of firsthand research.

EXAMPLE:

A diary entry would be the original (primary) work, and a book quoting the diary would be the secondary source.

NOTE: The information necessary for a citation for secondary source material can usually be found on the title page, verso, table of contents page, box/container, introductory/concluding frames, in accompanying documentation, reference materials, media, and/or on the item itself.

Book cited   1. J. C. Pillered, *An Economic History of*
in a book   *the Western World* (New York: Stock
                   Market Press, 1984), 31, cited in Harriet
                   Coyle, *Human Nature in Hard Economic*

Times (Chicago: Univ. of Chicago Press, 1994), 300.

NOTE: You are using the Coyle book and find the Pillered book quoted.

Book cited
in a magazine

2. George H. Abrams, *The History of the Arabian Horse in America* (New York: Wagoneer & Sons, 1976), 50–3, cited in Nellie Hesco, "Famous Breeding Mares," *Horseman's Journal*, July 1978, 17.

Newspaper
article cited
in a magazine

3. Barton Dempsey, "Political Corruption Exposed," *Tweedtown Standard* (DE), March 17, 1990, Sec. I, 1, cited in Mary Isabelle Longworth, "Politics and Values," *American Journal*, November, 1991, 80–1.

How Do You Write a Footnote Entry for an Adaptation?

This is a general guide for footnoting an ADAPTATION; however, THERE ARE MANY DIFFERENCES. Make sure you follow the specific examples. Condensed*/abridged* works are footnoted in the same manner as adaptations. The following forms are for both PRINTED and NONPRINT materials.

---

1. adapter's name, "adapted title" adaptation of "original title" [format] by author's name (place of publication of adapted work: publisher of adapted work, date of adaptation), page # [format].

NOTE: The information necessary for an adaptation citation can be found on the title page, verso, table of contents page, box/container, introductory/concluding frames, in reference materials, accompanying documentation, media, and/or on the item itself.

*These terms are defined in the glossary.

Short story adaptation of play	1. Sam States, "The Red, White, and Blue" adaptation of *Forever USA* [play] by Walter Nation (Philadelphia: Ben Franklin Press, 1986), 17 [short story].

NOTE: *Forever USA* is underlined because plays are underlined; short works are in quotation marks.

Motion picture/ video recording adaptation of a book	2. Betty Edsel, *Dynamite and Me* adaptation of *My Life With Peter* [book] by Mary Cohen (New York: Musical Theater Publications. 1954) [motion picture].

NOTE: *Dynamite and Me* is underlined because motion pictures are underlined.

Audio recording adaptation of poem	3. Molly Flagg, composer, "Stand Up" adaptation of "Love of Country" [poem] by Nathan Hancock (Boston: Key Studio, 1990) [audio disk, JAM 321].
Filmstrip adaptation of motion picture/ video recording	4. "Sea Flight" adaptation of *Country at War* [video recording] (Burbank: Flynn Films, 1993) [filmstrip].
Printed speech adaptation of a nonprint speech	5. Martha Roosevelt, "It's Time For a Woman" adaptation of "It's Time for a Woman" [TV—NBC] (Washington: Political Printers, 1994) [print speech].
Condensed work	6. Faith Hopeful, *A Midnight Ride* condensed version of *A Midnight Ride* [autobiography] by Charity W. Virtue (Juneau, AK: Platitude Press, 1985), 85 [biography].

Abridged work   7. Walter Brummel, *The Antique
                     Lover's Abridged Guide* abridged version
                     of *The Antique Lover's Guide* [book] by
                     Cassie Eastlake (Tarrytown, DE: Beau
                     Brothers, 1991), 21 [book].

Footnoting Nonprint Material

How Do You Write a Footnote Entry for a Filmstrip?

This is a general guide for footnoting a FILMSTRIP; however,
THERE ARE MANY DIFFERENCES. Make sure you follow the
specific examples. For ADAPTATIONS, see citations under
Adaptation.

---

1. author's name, "title of filmstrip" (producer/manufac-
turer, date of production manufacturer) [filmstrip].

NOTE: The information necessary for a filmstrip citation
        can usually be found on the introductory frames
        and/or the box or container.

Single filmstrip   1. Caesar Hannibal, "Historic Gaul"
with author   (Alpine Pictures, 1987) [filmstrip].

Single   2. "Costuming With Sacks" (Fifth
filmstrip with   Avenue Productions, 1989) [filmstrip].
no author

Filmstrip   3. Taylor Lord, "Loveseat Couches"
with author,   in *Interior Decorating,* (Ethan Allan
part of a set   Manufacturing, 1992) [filmstrip].

Filmstrip with   4. "Early American Coverlets" in
no author,   *Bedroom Decorating* (May Altmann
part of a set   Ideas, 1990) [filmstrip].

Set of filmstrips   5. Colleen Faust, *Office Procedures*
with author   (Beyer Maia Productions, 1993)
                        [filmstrip].

Set of filmstrips with no author	6. *Nocturnal Animals* (Science Concepts, 1991) [filmstrip].

How Do You Write a Footnote Entry for a Media Kit?

This is a general guide for footnoting a MEDIA KIT; however, you should follow the specific examples. For ADAPTATIONS, see citations under Adaptation.

A media kit is defined as two or more different nonprint media treated as one set, for example, a filmstrip and cassette.

---

1. author's name, *title of media kit* (producer/manufacturer, date of production/manufacture) [format].

NOTE: The information necessary for a media kit citation can usually be found on the container, in accompanying documentation, and/or on the individual item itself.

Media kit with author	1. C. Barr, *Candy Making* (Paul Peter's Productions, 1988) [2 filmstrips & 2 records].
Media kit with no author	2. *Salad Making* (Father Earth & Sons, 1992) [80 slides and cassette].

How Do You Write a Footnote Entry for a Motion Picture-Video Recording?

This is a general guide for footnoting a MOTION PICTURE-VIDEO RECORDING; however, THERE ARE MANY DIFFERENCES. Make sure you follow the specific examples. For ADAPTATIONS, see citations under Adaptation.

Motion pictures include feature-length films,* single-reel films,* film cartridges*/loops*; these can be 16 mm., 8 mm., and/or super 8 mm.

---

*These terms are defined in the glossary.

Video recording includes reel-to-reel videotapes,* videocassettes,* videodisks,* and television.

---

1. *title of item* (producer/manufacturer, date of production/manufacture) [format].

NOTE: The information necessary for a motion picture/video recording citation can usually be found on the introductory/concluding frames, accompanying documentation, and/or on the box or container.

Feature-length motion picture
: 1. *Cameo of a Comedian* (Hollywood Productions, 1991) [feature-length film].

Single-reel film
: 2. *Fun With Photography* (El Cine Releases, 1990) [single-reel film].

Film cartridge/loop
: 3. *The Comedic Fall* (Pratfall Releases, 1990) [film cartridge].

Reel-to-reel videotape
: 4. *Understanding the GNP* (Wall Street Publications, 1992) [videotape].

Videocassette
: 5. *How to Use a Computer* (Easy Learn Manufacturing, 1994) [videocassette].

Videodisk
: 6. *Daffodil in the Meadow* (Fleur Creations, 1993) [videodisk].

Video recording, part of a series
: 7. *American Stocks in a Bear Market* in *Economics for the Everyday Person* (Monetary Productions, 1989) [videocassette].

Television
: 8. *What Are We Going to Do With the Money?* (August 8, 1992) [TV—ABC].

*These terms are defined in the glossary.

How Do You Write a Footnote Entry for an Audio Recording?

This is a general guide for footnoting an AUDIO RECORDING; however, THERE ARE MANY DIFFERENCES. Make sure you follow the specific examples. For ADAPTATIONS, see citations under Adaptation.

Audio recordings include records, record albums, compact disks, audiocassettes*, audiodisks,* and reel-to-reel audiotapes.*

---

1. author's/composer's name, author/composer, *title of item* performer's/artist's/narrator's/reader's/commentator's name, performer/artist/narrator/reader/commentator (producer/manufacturer, date of production/manufacture) [format identification number].

NOTE: The information necessary for an audio recording citation can usually be found on the box or container and/or on the item itself.

Single record with author and reader	1. Sonny Sirocco, author, *Dust in The Wind Tales,* Connie Ellen Verbose, reader (Sweet Sounds, 1990) [audiodisk MU525].
Single record with no author/ composer	2. *Spring Raindrops* (Easy Records, 1982) [audiodisk NS417].
Single record with commentator and no author/ composer	3. *Weather and Energy: A Team* Gayle Whyte, commentator (Mark Media, 1992) [audiodisk PCO788].
Record album with artist	4. *The Shakespearean Histories* Sir Oliver Laurence, artist (Bacon Manufacturers, 1990) [album 941VBG].

*These terms are defined in the glossary.

Single cassette with composer	5. T. Storm, composer, *An Avalanche of Love* (Mountain Melodies, 1994) [audiocassette PUL994].
Single cassette with composer and artist	6. Star B. Cumulus, composer, *Clouds in the Heavens* Misty M. Martin, artist (Castover Productions, 1989) [audiocassette PUB86].
Single cassette with narrator, part of a set	7. *Stories for a Rainy Evening* Sonny Dusk, narrator, in *Nighttime Tales* (Weatherson, 1992) [audiocassette WTZ344].
Set of cassettes with author/composer	8. Stormy Days, author, *The Complete Collection of Weather Stories Throughout the World* (Wind Ridge Records, 1986) [3 audiocassettes HN546].
Set of cassettes with no author/composer	9. *Laboratory Safety* (Sims Labs, 1990) [5 audiocassettes ECOS12].
Reel-to-reel tape with no author/composer	10. *Sounds of Weather* (Scud Releases, 1991) [audiotape TDB986].
Compact disk with artist	11. *Candlelight Memories* Julio Placido, artist (Wax Productions, 1994) [compact disk NAS417].

How Do You Write a Footnote Entry for Computer Software?

This is a general guide for footnoting COMPUTER SOFTWARE; however, THERE ARE MANY DIFFERENCES. Make sure you follow the specific examples.

Computer software includes diskettes,* tapes,* disks,* and CD-ROM.*

*These terms are defined in the glossary.

> 1. "title of program" program writer's name (producer/
> manufacturer, date of production/manufacture) [format].

NOTE: The information necessary for a computer software
        citation can usually be found on the introductory
        frames of the program, on the box or container, in
        the accompanying documentation, and/or on the
        item itself.

Diskette with program writer*	1. "Word Derivatives" Nicholas W. Fig (Charles Hardson, 1993) [diskette].
Diskette with no program writer	2. "Vocabulary Study for the GRE" (Lerose Com-u-ed, 1994) [diskette & manual].
Diskette with program writer, part of a set	3. "Compound Interest" Penelope O'Rourke in *Business Math Problems* (Pascal Associates, 1993) [diskette & manual].
Tape with program writer	4. "The Inventory Master" Ronald Van Dyke (Count Creations, 1994) [computer tape].
Tape with no program writer	5. "Measuring As a Life Skill" (Kirt Products, 1993) [computer tape].
Disk with program writer	6. "The Complete Library System" Dewey Archibald (Circulation Systems, 1992) [computer disk & manual].
Disk with no program writer	7. "The American Record Keeper" (Data Enterprises, 1994) [computer disk & manual].

*These terms are defined in the glossary.

CD-ROM   8. "Authors of New England"
                    (Hawthorne/Emerson, 1994) [CD-ROM].

How Do You Write a Footnote Entry for a Microscope Slide?

This is a general guide for footnoting a MICROSCOPE SLIDE; however, THERE ARE MANY DIFFERENCES. Make sure you follow the specific examples.

---

1. "title/subject of the slide" (producer/manufacturer, date of production/manufacture) [microscope slide].

NOTE: The information necessary for a microscope slide citation can usually be found on the box or container and/or on the slide itself.

Single slide   1. "Paramecium" (Barry Clement, 1986) [microscope slide].

Single slide,   2. "Seaweed Reproduction" in *Marine*
part of a set   *Organisms* (Fischer & Sons, 1991) [microscope slide].

Set of slides   3. *Fresh Water Protozoa* (O'Gorman Scientific Supply House, 1989) [microscope slide].

How Do You Write a Footnote Entry for a Photographic Slide?

This is a general guide for footnoting a PHOTOGRAPHIC SLIDE; however, THERE ARE MANY DIFFERENCES. Make sure you follow the specific examples.

---

1. photographer's name, "title/subject of the slide" (producer/manufacturer, date of production/manufacture) [photographic slide].

NOTE: The information necessary for a photographic slide citation can usually be found on the box or container and/or on the slide itself.

Single slide   1. Patrick Parsons, "Friar Ambrose"
with   (Art International, 1985) [photographic
photographer   slide].

Single slide   2. "Mob violence" (Associated Press,
with no   1989) [untitled photographic slide].
photographer

NOTE: When a photographic slide is untitled, describe it briefly, indicating any information that might be available on its origin.

Single slide   1. Harold Gardener, "Daisy" in *Flowers*
with   *of North America* (Botany, 1991) [photo-
photographer,   graphic slide].
part of a set

Set of slides   2. *America's Cartoonists* (Appalachia
                             Slides, 1989) [photographic slide].

How Do You Write a Footnote Entry for a Photograph?

This is a general guide for footnoting a PHOTOGRAPH; however, THERE ARE MANY DIFFERENCES. Make sure you follow the specific examples.

---

1. photographer's name, "title/subject of the photograph" (producer/manufacturer, date of production/manufacture) [photograph].

NOTE: The information necessary for a photograph citation can usually be found on the box or container and/or on the photograph itself.

Single photograph with photographer	1. Felix Trousseau, "The Wedding Ceremony" (Oxford, 1987) [photograph].
Single photograph with no photographer or title	2. "Abandoned child crying on railroad platform" (n.d.) [untitled photograph].

NOTE: When a photograph is untitled, describe it briefly, indicating any information that might be available on its origin.

Single photograph with photographer, part of a set	3. F.W. Daggeur, "Old woman with a bird" in *Aging* (Seniors Plus, 1990) [untitled photograph].
Set of photographs	4. Albert Prince, *Clothing Styles of the Decade* (Ascot, 1991) [photograph].

How Do You Write a Footnote Entry for a Transparency?

This is a general guide for footnoting a TRANSPARENCY; however, THERE ARE MANY DIFFERENCES. Make sure you follow the specific examples.

---

1. producer/manufacturer, "title/subject of the transparency" (producer/manufacturer, date of production/manufacture) [transparency].

NOTE: The information necessary for a transparency citation can usually be found on the box or container and/or on the transparency itself.

Single transparency with producer	1. Agatha Fulcy, "Job Outlook in the Year 2010" (Projections All, 1994) [transparency].
Single transparency with no creator or title	2. "Red color shades" (Scarlet Tones, 1990) [untitled transparency].

NOTE: When a transparency is untitled, describe it briefly, indicating any information that might be available on its origin.

Single transparency with producer, part of a set	3. Abu Zaka, "Somalia" in *Maps of the Dark Continent* (Abu Zaka, 1994) [transparency].
Set of transparencies	4. *Media References* (Instructional Services, 1994) [transparency].

How Do You Write a Footnote Entry for a Radio Broadcast?

This is a general guide for footnoting a RADIO BROADCAST; however, THERE ARE MANY DIFFERENCES. Make sure you follow the specific examples. For ADAPTATIONS see citations under Adaptation.

---

1. "title of individual broadcast" broadcaster's name, broadcaster (date of broadcast) [radio—station/network].

NOTE: The information necessary for a radio broadcast citation can usually be found in the newspaper listings for the broadcast or taken from the broadcast itself.

Single broadcast	1. "The Abortion Amendment" Leo E. Boynton, broadcaster (November 2, 1994) [radio—KDKA].

Single broadcast, part of a series	2. "Interviews With the Candidates" Netty Kay Speaker, broadcaster (January 6, 1987) part of *America Wants to Know* [radio—WABC].
Series of broadcasts	3. *Political Problems of the United Nations* James R. Banner, broadcaster (May 14 to July 13, 1994) [radio—WNYC].

How Do You Write a Footnote Entry for a Piece of Realia?

This is a general guide for footnoting a piece of REALIA; however, THERE ARE MANY DIFFERENCES. Make sure you follow the specific examples.

Realia is defined as real or reproduced articles used to enhance classroom instruction, for example, primitive tools, medieval costumes, rock specimens, or ancient coins.

---

1. *title/subject of piece* (producer/manufacturer/collector, date of production/manufacture/origin) [realia].

NOTE: The information necessary for a realia citation can usually be found on the box or container. Some of the information may not be available.

Commercially produced realia	1. *Tools of the Aztecs* (Summerfall-Winterspring Productions, 1994) [realia].
Organization's collection of realia	2. *New York State Rocks* (New York State Geological Association Museum, 1991) [realia].
Individual's unlabeled collection of realia	3. *Commemorative stamps of U.S. Presidents* (Alfred F. EIhu, n.d.) [unlabeled realia].

NOTE: If there is no information on the box or container, provide your own title.

How Do You Write a Footnote Entry for a Nonprint Speech, Lecture, or Sermon?

This is a general guide for footnoting a nonprint SPEECH, LEC-TURE, or SERMON; however, THERE ARE MANY DIFFER-ENCES. Make sure you follow the specific examples. For ADAPTATIONS, see citations under Adaptation. The form below is for a NONPRINT speech, lecture, or sermon; for a PRINTED speech, lecture, or sermon, see citations in the printed materials section.

A nonprint speech, lecture, or sermon is defined as an oral message given before an audience for a specific purpose.

---

1. speaker's name, identification of speaker, "title/subject of speech/lecture/sermon" (location of speech/lecture/sermon, date of speech/lecture/sermon) [format].

NOTE: The information necessary for a nonprint speech, lecture, or sermon citation can usually be found in accompanying documentation or obtained at the time of the speech/lecture/sermon.

Classroom lecture	1. Joseph Balboa, Professor of History, "American Explorations" (Pioneer Univ., November 26, 1992) [classroom lecture].
Political speech	2. Senator Paula Harangue, Chairwoman of Rules Committee, "Reelection" (Civic Auditorium, October 30, 1993) [political speech].
Formal report	3. Edward Conduit, Chairman of Citizens Water Treatment Committee,

"Safe Water" (Council Chambers,
September 20, 1992) [formal report].

Commencement 4. Jennifer Patrick, Dean of Students at
address Gerrard College, "Keeping Up With the
Joneses" (Academy of Fashion &
Design, August 17, 1993) [commence-
ment address].

Sermon 5. Ambrose Kierns, M.M., Maryknoll
Missionary, "His Power" (Bethany
Church, March 22, 1993) [sermon].

NOTE: This form is used when the writer is *physically present* at the speech/lecture/sermon.

Speech on TV 6. David E. James, Political Analyst,
"The 1984 Presidential Primary" taken
from *CBS Election Report* (April 3, 1984)
[TV—CBS].

Sermon on 7. Judith A. Leopold, Minister at Trinity
radio Cathedral, "Baptism Gives New Life"
taken from *Sunday Morning Speaks*
(February 29, 1996) [radio—WHUD].

How Do You Write a Footnote Entry for Nonprint Conference, Convention, or Seminar Proceedings?

This is a general guide for footnoting a live or video CONFERENCE, CONVENTION, or SEMINAR. For the transcript of a conference, convention, or seminar, see citations in the printed materials section.

A nonprint conference, convention, or seminar is defined as live or video proceedings of a conference, convention, or seminar.

---

1. sponsoring organization's name, "title of conference/
convention/seminar" (location of conference/convention/
seminar, date of conference/convention, seminar) [format].

NOTE: The information necessary for the live or video proceedings of a conference/convention/seminar can usually be found in accompanying documentation or obtained at the time of the conference/convention/seminar.

Live conference/
convention/
seminar
proceedings

1. Health Benefits International, "Controlling Prices" (London, October, 1994) [conference].

Video
conference/
convention/
seminar
proceedings

2. Murphy Fire Installations, "New Fire Codes" (Yonkers, NY, February 1995) [video seminar].

How Do You Write a Footnote Entry for a Distance Learning Presentation?

This is a general guide for footnoting a DISTANCE LEARNING presentation.

1. "title of individual presentation," name of course, name of presenter, identification of presenter (date of transmission) transmission location [distance learning—format].

NOTE: The information for a distance learning presentation can usually be found in accompanying documentation or obtained at the time of the presentation.

Distance
learning via
television

1. "The Habitats of Gorillas," Advanced Biology, Stacey Hodge, teacher (March 21, 1995) Brewster, NY [distance learning—TV].

Distance learning via radio	2. "Australia's Early Inhabitants— Aborigines," Australian History. Melba Simpson, lecturer (September 1, 1996) Alice Springs, Austr. [distance learning—radio].

How Do You Write a Footnote Entry for a Nonprint Interview?

This is a general guide for footnoting a nonprint INTERVIEW; however, THERE ARE MANY DIFFERENCES. Make sure you follow the specific examples. The form below is for a NONPRINT interview; for a PRINTED interview, see citations in the printed materials section.

---

1. interviewee's name, identification of interviewee, interviewed by interviewer's name, "subject/title of interview" (location of interview, date of interview).

NOTE: The information necessary for a nonprint interview citation can usually be obtained at the time of the interview.

Personal interview	1. Jerome King, Sportscaster, interviewed by Julianna F. Kimberly, "College Recruitment" (Memorial Stadium, January 6, 1992).

NOTE: This form is used when the writer is *physically present*, i.e., conducting the interview or observing it firsthand.

Interview on TV	2. Mikel Jon Miceli, Italian Ambassador, interviewed by Patsy Fosina, "Italian-American Economic Relationship" taken from *Meet the Press* (October 2, 1994) [TV—CBS].

Interview   3. Josephine Harrison, Career
on radio   Consultant, interviewed by Kelliann
                   Roberts, "Networking" taken from
                   Weekend Job Market (April 11, 1993)
                   [radio—WPUT].

NOTE: If an interview is untitled, provide your own title
        based on the subject.

How Do You Write a Footnote Entry for a Microform?

This is a general guide for footnoting a MICROFORM; however,
THERE ARE MANY DIFFERENCES. Make sure you follow the
specific examples.

Microform includes microfilm* and microfiche.*

---

1. author's name, *title of microfilm/microfiche* (producer/
manufacturer, date of production/manufacture) [format
identification number].

NOTE: The information necessary for a microform citation
        can usually be found on the container and/or on
        the item itself. Not all microforms have identifica-
        tion numbers.

Microfilm   1. Sigmund Fleischhauer, M.D., *The
with author   Effects of Microwaves on the Unborn*
                   (Microfilms of Canada, 1989) [microfilm
                   35-1625].

Microfiche   2. *Report of the President's Commission on
with no author   Curriculum Development in Health* (Univ.
                   of Colorado, 1990) [microfiche ERIC
                   Document ED 525 137].

*These terms are defined in the glossary.

Microfiche with no author, part of a set	3. *Genealogical Records of the Timoney Family* in *Families of Ireland* (Univ. of Donegal, 1990) [microfiche 6 27 56].

How Do You Write a Footnote Entry for Creative Arts?

This is a general guide for footnoting the CREATIVE ARTS; however, THERE ARE MANY DIFFERENCES. Make sure you follow the specific examples. For a type of artistic work not given here, use the basic form in the box.

Creative arts include sculpture, paintings, blueprints, musical compositions, etc.

---

1. creator's name, *title/subject of work* (date) [format].

NOTE: The information necessary for a creative arts citation can usually be found in the accompanying documentation or on the item itself.

Sculpture	1. Luigi Vincenzo, *Mother and Child* (1894) [sculpture].
Painting	2. C. Jolly Roger, *Sailing the Blue Horizon* (1839) [painting].
Blueprint	3. Blaise Moody, *Fine Arts Hall of New Mexico* (1985) [blueprint].
Musical composition	4. Wilhelmina Firman, *Mein Deutschland* (1942) [musical composition].
Single musical work	5. Nelson Debs, "The March of the Green Bears" (1980) [musical composition].
Single work as part of a	6. April Mars, "Jumping Jupiter" in *The Heavenly Planets Serenade* (1968)

longer musical composition	[musical composition].

How Do You Write a Footnote Entry for a Telephone/Conference Call?

This is a general guide for footnoting a TELEPHONE/CONFER-ENCE CALL.

> 1. name of person(s) called, identification of person(s) called called by a caller's name, "subject of telephone/con-ference call (date of telephone/conference call).

NOTE: The information necessary for a telephone/confer-ence call citation can be obtained at the time of the call.

Telephone call	1. Peter Kilcommons, Business Manager of North United School District, called by Mary Northrup, "Employee Assistance Program" (May 15, 1993).
Conference call	2. Board of Trustees, Brewster Teachers' Welfare Fund, called by John Fischer, "Benefit Updates" (June 19, 1994).

Bibliography

What is a Bibliography?

A standard bibliography is a listing of the materials used in a research/term paper. A supplementary bibliography is a listing of the materials referred to but not used.

When is a Bibliography Used?

A bibliography is used in every research/term paper.

What Types of Bibliography are Used for a Research/Term Paper?

There are four types of bibliography for a research/term paper:

1. preliminary
2. working
3. standard
4. supplementary

1. A *preliminary bibliography* is used to determine if there is enough material available on a subject. This is done prior to starting formal research.
2. A *working bibliography* is used while gathering information and writing the paper.
3. A *standard bibliography* is the final listing of the materials actually cited in the paper.

4. A *supplementary bibliography* is a listing of the materials referred to but not actually cited in the paper. This is an optional listing.

Do not confuse these bibliographies with an ANNOTATED BIBLIOGRAPHY, which is a listing of explanatory or critical notes and comments on a work. See sample in the Appendix.

Should Bibliographic Entries be Numbered?

No, bibliographic entries are arranged alphabetically by the author's last name or, if no author is given, by the first word of the title.

Must the Author's Full Name be Rewritten for Each of His or Her Works Listed in a Bibliography?

No, in the second and subsequent citations, the author's name may be indicated by a straight line approximately ten characters in length. In such cases materials are listed alphabetically by the first word of the title unless, of course, it is "A," "An," or "The."

EXAMPLE:

> Richards, Jonathan. *Egypt: Land of Enchantment*. London: Oxland Press, 1995.
> _____. *The Islamic Nations*. London: St. James Publications, 1988.
> _____. *Nile, A River of Mystery*. London: Oxland Press, 1986.

Are There Shortened Terms That Can Be Used in a Bibliography?

Yes, the shortened terms are the same as those used for footnotes. Refer to this question in the footnote section.

When using any of these shortened terms in footnotes, also use the applicable ones in bibliographic entries. Be consistent throughout the paper.

What Do Sample Bibliographic Entries Look Like?

BIBLIOGRAPHY

Bingham, Isaiah. *Women of New England*. Boston: Peabody Press, 1985.

Caruthers, Benjamin. *The History of New Bedford*. Springfield, MA: Ahab & Son, 1990.

Herman, Dick. *Massachusetts Memoirs*. Cambridge: Crimson Press, MA: 1902.

Rivers, Seaman. *Why Whaling?* Boston: Melville Books, 1899.

Waters, Ishmael. *Moby and Friends*. New York: Harpoon Press, 1888.

Where Does a Bibliography Appear in a Research/Term Paper?

The bibliography comes at the end of a paper; it may either precede or follow the appendix, if there is one. The bibliography begins on a separate page with its centered heading on the first page only. APA style also uses this placement.

If a supplementary bibliography is included, it, too, begins on a separate page with its own centered heading on the first page only. A supplementary bibliography immediately follows the standard bibliography.

Entries for Printed Material

How Do You Write a Bibliographic Entry for a Book?

This is a general guide for a bibliographic entry for a BOOK; however, THERE ARE MANY DIFFERENCES. Make sure you follow the specific examples. For ADAPTATIONS, see citations under Adaptation.

Reference books such as dictionaries, atlases, almanacs, manuals, and handbooks follow the sample in the box. Specific examples of some of the most commonly used reference books are also included.

author's last name, first name. *title of book*. place of publication: publisher, date of publication.

NOTE: The information necessary for a book citation can be found on the title page and/or verso.

Book with one author	Johnson, Sam. *The Memoirs of Frannie Lapp*. Houston: Monkey Press, 1989.
Book with two authors	Tishner, Marvin and Bernard Schwartz. *Colored Prism: Hues of Green*. New York: Large Press, 1988.

NOTE: "Hues of Green" is a subtitle separated from the title by a colon.

Book with three authors	Oates, Ray, Edwin Barley, & Gerald Rye. *Wheat for the World*. San Diego: Clyde Colt & Sons, 1991.
Book with more than three authors	Ashbridge, Nia & others. *Tracing Your English Ancestors*. New York: Blackcourt, 1990.

OR

Ashbridge, Nia, et al. *Tracing Your English Ancestors*. New York: Blackcourt, 1990.

Book with association/ institution as author	American Media Association. *Guide to Media Centers*. Chicago: American Media Association, 1988.
Book with no author	*Images on the Water*. Seaton, MS: D. Pierce, 1980.

Book with editor and author	Moose, Richard Erwin. *The History of Livingston County*. Ed. by Edward M. Cox. Rochester, NY: Genesee Press, 1987.
Book with editor and no author	Pine, Judy, ed. *Great Trees of North America*. Dallas: Greenleaf & Trunk, 1992.
Book with compiler and no author	Reynard, Geraldine, comp. *Thrift Shops in New England*. Springtown, NH: Penrose, 1990.
Book with author and translator	Chips, Everett. *Troubleshooting Computers*. trans. by Erin DeLuca. Danbury, CT: Hatter Press, 1994.
Book with translator and no author	Gundermodd, Edward D., trans. *Treatises from the Roman Courts*. Rome: Italian Press, 1987.
Dictionary	Thornton, E. L., ed. *Thornton Dictionary*, 4th ed. Peoria, IL: Johnson Southerby, 1994.
Atlas	*Great World Atlas*, 5th ed. Wappingers Falls, NY: Hopewell Press, 1995.
Almanac	"Education: New Jersey." *Reader's 1995 Almanac*. Paterson, NJ: Trenton Releases, 1995.

How Do You Write a Bibliographic Entry for a Pamphlet?

This is a general guide for a bibliographic entry for a PAMPHLET; however, THERE ARE MANY DIFFERENCES. Make sure you follow the specific examples.

> author's last name, first name. *title of pamphlet.* place of publication: publisher, date of publication.

NOTE:	The information necessary for a pamphlet citation can be found on the front cover, title page, verso, inside back cover, back cover, and/or last page of the pamphlet. Some of the information may not be available.

Pamphlet with author	Housing, Paul. *Revitalizing the Inner City.* Detroit: Committee for Social Improvement, 1992.
Pamphlet with no author	*Plague.* Washington: U.S. Government Printing Office, 1989.
Pamphlet with association/ institution as author	Committee on Fair Labor Practices. *The Effect of Bankruptcy on Negotiating a Union Contract.* Washington: American Federation of Union Breakers, 1994.

How Do You Write a Bibliographic Entry for an Encyclopedia Article?

This is a general guide for a bibliographic entry for an ENCYCLOPEDIA ARTICLE; however, THERE ARE MANY DIFFERENCES. Make sure you follow the specific examples.

> article author's last name, first name. "title of article." *name of encyclopedia.* date of publication. volume #/letter.

NOTE:	The information necessary for an encyclopedia article citation can be found on the title page, verso of the specific volume used (or of the first volume of the set or of the index volume), and/or on the article itself.

Signed encyclopedia article	Brown, William J. "Twentieth Century Architecture." *Encyclopedia Americana*. 1991. XXVI.
Unsigned encyclopedia article	"Dogs." *Encyclopaedia Britannica*. 1994. IV.
Signed encyclopedia article in yearbook	Greene, Guy. "Hot Air Balloons." *The 1992 World Book Year Book*. 1992.
Unsigned encyclopedia article in one-volume encyclopedia	"Computers." *Columbia Encyclopedia*. 5th ed. 1990.

How Do You Write a Bibliographic Entry for a Magazine Article?

This is a general guide for a bibliographic entry for a MAGAZINE ARTICLE; however, THERE ARE MANY DIFFERENCES. Make sure you follow the specific examples.

---

article author's last name, first name. "title/headline of article." *name of magazine*. date of magazine.

NOTE:	The information necessary for a magazine article citation can be found on the table of contents page, editorial page, and/or on the specific article being used.
Signed article	Grumet, B. "The Law and the Battered Child." *PTA Magazine*. December 1990.
Unsigned article	"Caps for Christmas." *The Bottle Capper* (IA). October 1983.

NOTE: If the magazine is not generally known, the state is put in parentheses following the name of the magazine.

Signed   Boone, Herbert. "There Is Fairness." Rev.
review   of *Discrimination* (Genesee Press) by
with   William Whimper. In *Sports*
title   *Illustrated*. February 17, 1992.

NOTE: Following the title of the review indicate the name of the work being reviewed, its publisher/producer and/or author.

Signed   Holbine, Martha. Rev. of "Primary
review with   Spotlight" (NBC). In *The Maine Sun*.
no title   August 17, 1994.

Editorial with   "Jimmy Jock." Editorial. *Sport*.
title   August 17, 1993.

Editorial   Editorial. *Mademoiselle*. April 1991.
with no title

NOTE: Since most editorials are unsigned, the bibliographic entry begins with the editorial title, if given. If no title is indicated, begin the entry with the word "Editorial."

Signed column   Ways, Bill. "Ramblings." Column. *Travel*
with title   *Lore*. May 8, 1994.

Signed   Fine, Mike. Column. *World of Stereo*. July
column with   1993.
no title

How Do You Write a Bibliographic Entry for a Newspaper Article?

This is a general guide for a bibliographic entry for a NEWSPAPER ARTICLE; however, THERE ARE MANY DIFFERENCES. Make sure you follow the specific examples.

> article author's last name, first name. "title/headline of arti-
> cle." *name of newspaper*. date of newspaper.

NOTE: The information necessary for a newspaper article citation can be found on the table of contents page, editorial page, and/or on the specific article being used.

Signed article   Ambrose, Joseph. "Riot Erupts in Capital City." *Boonetown Standard* (TN). December 1, 1991.

NOTE: If the newspaper is not generally known, the state is put in parentheses following the name of the newspaper.

Unsigned article   "Pilgrims Flock to Jerusalem." *The Jerusalem Post*. June 22, 1994.

Signed review with title   Edwards, Joseph. "The Wee Asp." Rev. of "Gidget Goes Boston" (Bombast Films). *The New England Weekly*. March 21, 1965.

NOTE: Following the title of the review indicate the name of the work being reviewed, its publisher/producer and/or author.

Signed review with no title   Critic, Cora. Rev. of *Modern Shakespeare* (Billboard Press) by Richard Old. *New Republic*. March 21, 1993.

Editorial with title   "Where's the Water?" Editorial. *Arizona Pioneer*. July 3, 1990.

Editorial with no title   Editorial. *London Messenger*. May 25, 1993.

NOTE: Since most editorials are unsigned, the biblio-
        graphic entry begins with the editorial title, if
        given. If no title is indicated, begin the entry with
        the word "Editorial."

Signed   Kohan, Mary. "As I Was Saying . . ."
column   Column. *Bronx Review*. September
with title   11, 1992.

Signed   Martyr, Marlene. Column. *Sioux City*
column   *Press*. August 25, 1994.
with no title

How Do You Write a Bibliographic Entry for a Poem?

This is a general guide for a bibliographic entry for a POEM; however, THERE ARE MANY DIFFERENCES. Make sure you follow
the specific examples. For ADAPTATIONS, see citations under
Adaptation.

---

author's last name, first name. "title of poem." place of pub-
    lication: publisher, date of publication.

NOTE: The information necessary for a poetic citation can
        be found on the title page, verso, table of contents
        page, editorial page, and/or on the poem itself.

Single   Billowy, Robert. "Ode to the Spanish
poem   Sails." San Jose, CA: Nautical Press,
                        1980.

Anonymous   "Night of the Knight." Camelot, Eng.:
poem   Stillwell & Sons, 1985.

Poem in an   MacKeel, Scotty. "Loch Ness Me."
anthology/   Quoted in *Scotland's Heritage*.
collection   Lansing, MI: Edinboro Publications,
by author   1991.

Poem in an anthology/ collection with an editor	Dewy, Susan J. "Ballad of the Rain." Quoted by Thomas Weatherbee, ed., in *Rainbow Lyrics*. Sun City, FL: Solar & Sons, 1990.
Poem in an anthology/ collection with a compiler	Deisel, Angelo. "People of Germany." Quoted by Charles Vaughan, comp., in *Poems of the World*. Pontiac, NV: Kutchman & Son, 1986.
Poem in a periodical	Von Pelt, Monica. "Warm Fuzzies." Quoted in *Furtrappers' Monthly* (SD). December 1988.

How Do You Write a Bibliographic Entry for a Play?

This is a general guide for a bibliographic entry for a PLAY; however, THERE ARE MANY DIFFERENCES. Make sure you use the specific examples. For ADAPTATIONS, see citations under Adaptation.

---

author's last name, first name. *title of play*, place of publication: publisher, date of publication.

NOTE: The information necessary for a play citation can be found on the title page, verso, table of contents page, editorial page, and/or on the play itself.

Single play	Handsome, William. *The Raising of My Father*. Padre, NM: Pops Press, 1990.
Anonymous play	*Seagulls on the Waterfront*. Bayonne, NJ: Bird-Sky Prints, 1991.
One-act play	Matson, Jeannette. *Truth*. Honesty, WV: Purity Publications, 1993.

Play in an anthology/ collection by author	Cammarosano, Linda. *Our Campaigning Horizon*. Quoted in *On the Political Side of Life*. Albany, NY: Tom Sander Associates, 1994.
Play in an anthology/ collection with an editor	Wordsmith, Wenda. *One Sparkling Moment*. Quoted by I. Penworth, ed., in *Plays for a Romantic Evening*. San Diego: Dramatic Press, 1989.
Play in an anthology/ collection with a compiler	Floral, George. *Tulip Time*. Quoted by Rose Arbor, comp., in *Blossoming Freedoms*. Garden City, NY: Horticultural Press, 1992.
Play in a periodical	Breakage, Libby. *Keys of Glass*. Quoted in *Interpretive Plays*. September 1992.

How Do You Write a Bibliographic Entry for a Short Story?

This is a general guide for a bibliographic entry for a SHORT STORY; however, THERE ARE MANY DIFFERENCES. Make sure you follow the specific examples. For ADAPTATIONS, see citations under Adaptation.

> author's last name, first name. "title of short story." place of publication: publisher, date of publication.

NOTE: The information necessary for a short story citation can be found on the title page, verso, table of contents page, editorial page, and/or on the story itself.

Single short story	Blaque, Scarlet. "Artist's Palette." Red Hook, MT: Crimson Press, 1988.
Short story in anthology/ collection by author	Browne, Etan. "Blew Prism." Quoted in *Kaleidoscope Memories*. Orange Oaks, NJ: Hue & Son, 1994.

Short story in anthology/ collection with an editor	Blanc, Terra. "Ebony." Quoted by Herbert Canarie, ed., in *Verde's Mountain*. Black Hills, ND: Yelo-Press Publications, 1991.
Short story in anthology/ collection with a compiler	Rouge, Elicia. "Lilac Nights." Quoted by Frances Whyte, comp., in *Horizons Forever*. Denville, TX: Rainbow Press, 1990.
Short story in a periodical	Fields, Grey. "Mother's Colorful Childhood." Quoted in *The Artists' Family Journal* (RI). June 1991.

How Do You Write a Bibliographic Entry for an Essay?

This is a general guide for a bibliographic entry for an ESSAY; however, THERE ARE MANY DIFFERENCES. Make sure you follow the specific examples. For ADAPTATIONS, see citations under Adaptation.

> author's last name, first name. "title of essay." place of publication: publisher, date of publication.

NOTE: The information necessary for an essay citation can be found on the title page, verso, table of contents page, editorial page, and/or on the essay itself.

Single essay	McKiernan, Allegro. "Soothing Sounds." Nyack, NY: Andante Composers, 1993.
Anonymous essay	"Brother Is Ever-Present." Wichita, KS: All Eyes Press, 1994.
Essay in an anthology/ collection by author	Frank, Hamilton. "Colonial Rights." Quoted in *Revolutionary Times*. Philadelphia: Underdog Publications, 1970.

Essay in an anthology/ collection with an editor	Cice, Stanley. "Always Alibiing." Quoted by Robbyn Hallett, ed., in *Excuses Anonymous*. Brewster, MA: My-Time Press, 1989.
Essay in an anthology/ collection with a compiler	Elh, Ernestine. "Germanic Arts." Quoted by Evelyn Anders, comp., in *European Art Treasures*. Florence, It: Franco & Franco, 1991.
Essay in a periodical	Samuels, Sylvian. "Nature's Bounty." Quoted in *Eastern Evergreen* (NH). October 1990.

How Do You Write a Bibliographic Entry for the Transcript of a Speech, Lecture, or Sermon?

This is a general guide for a bibliographic entry for a printed SPEECH, LECTURE, or SERMON; however, THERE ARE MANY DIFFERENCES. Make sure you use the specific examples. For ADAPTATIONS, see citations under Adaptation. The form below is for a PRINTED speech, lecture, or sermon; for a NONPRINT speech, lecture, or sermon see citations in the nonprint section.

The transcript of a speech, lecture, or sermon is defined as a written message given to an individual or audience for a specific purpose.

---

speaker's last name, first name. Identification of speaker. "title of speech/lecture/sermon" place of publication: publisher, date of publication [format].

NOTE: The information necessary for a printed speech, lecture, or sermon citation can be found on the title can be found on the title page, verso, table of contents page, editorial page, and/or on the speech/lecture/sermon itself.

Single speech/ lecture/ sermon	Bradley, B.A. Pastor of Stone Heights Chapel. "Religious Resurrection" El, Ger.: Annunciation Publications, 1985 [sermon].
Anonymous speech/ lecture/sermon	"On Wings of Angels." Sault Saint Marie, MI: Archangel Publications, December 25, 1991 [sermon].
Speech/ lecture/ sermon in anthology/ collection by author	Pulse, Reymon, M.D. Chief of Medical Services at Getwel Hospital. "Effects of Nuclear Radiation on Brain Cells." Quoted in *Pulse's Essays on Nuclear Medicine*. Grosse Point, MI: Medical Arts, 1993 [lecture].
Speech/ lecture/ sermon in anthology/ collection with an editor	Mith, Pamela. Curator of Medieval Museum. "Unicorns: Fact or Fiction?" Quoted by Bobbi Ballad, ed., in *Animals in Legend*. Whitehorse, MT: Fantasy Fiction, 1993 [speech].
Speech/ lecture/ sermon in anthology/ collection with a compiler	Shampoo, Elsie. Cosmetology Instructor at Technical Trades. "Cutting Techniques." Quoted by Nancy Browne, comp., in *Modern Hair*. Los Angeles: Cosmo Paperbacks, 1992 [lecture].
Speech/ lecture/ sermon in a periodical	Summ, William. Economist. "The Wall Street Bulls and Bears." Quoted in *American Pauper* (NY). July 17, 1985 [speech].

How Do You Write a Bibliographic Entry for the Transcript of a Conference, Convention, or Seminar?

This is a general guide for a bibliographic entry for the transcript of a CONFERENCE, CONVENTION, or SEMINAR. For a live or video conference, convention, or seminar, see citations in the non-print section.

The transcript of a conference, convention, or seminar is defined as the written record of such proceedings.

> sponsoring organization's name. "title of conference/convention/seminar." place of publication: publisher, date of publication [format].

NOTE: The information necessary for conference/convention or seminar proceedings can be found on the title page, verso, or table of contents page.

Conference/	American Association of Cable
convention/	Networks. "Visions for the 21st
seminar	Century." Atlanta: American
proceedings	Association of Cable Networks,
	September 1994 [convention].

How Do You Write a Bibliographic Entry for the Transcript of an Interview?

This is a general guide for a bibliographic entry for a printed INTERVIEW; however, THERE ARE MANY DIFFERENCES. Make sure you follow the specific examples. The form below is for a PRINTED interview; for a NONPRINT interview, see citations in the nonprint section.

> interviewee's last name, first name. Identification of interviewee. Interviewed by interviewer's name. "title/subject of interview." date of interview. Quoted by compiler's/editor's name, comp./ed., in *title of book/periodical*. place of publication: publisher, date of publication.

NOTE: The information necessary for an interview cita-
         tion can be found on the title page, verso, table of
         contents page, editorial page, and/or on the inter-
         view itself.

Interview in an anthology/ collection with an editor	Starlet, Sally. Actress. Interviewed by Sue Leffler. "Stardom Is Not Roses." February 23, 1990. Quoted by Virginia N. Starr, ed., in *Meet the Celebrities*. Media, PA: Thalberg Publishing, 1991.
Interview in an anthology/ collection with a compiler	Homberg, H. Harold. U.N. Delegate from Great Britain. Interviewed by Martin Kope. "H. Harold Homberg." November 11, 1991. Quoted by Jon X. Mather, comp., in *Contemporary Statesmen*. New York: Plaza Publications, 1993.
Interview in a periodical	Doubleday, Jacques. Olympic Medalist. Interviewed by Mahre Caruthers. "Living Skis." January 27, 1993. Quoted in *Sporting Monthly*. February 1993.

NOTE: If an interview is untitled, provide your own title
         based on the subject.

How Do You Write a Bibliographic Entry for a Biblical Reference?

This is a general guide for a bibliographic entry for a BIBLICAL
REFERENCE. Make sure you follow the specific examples.

Name of book. book number. chapter: verse(s).

NOTE: The information necessary for a biblical citation
         can be found on the beginning page of the specific

book being used (for book number and name), on the top of the page containing the material (for chapter), and before the specific verse(s).

| Numbered book | Kings. I. 9:5–8. |

| Unnumbered book | Mark. 9:23. |

How Do You Write a Bibliographic Entry for a Document, Questionnaire, or Survey?

This is a general guide for a bibliographic entry for a DOCU-MENT, QUESTIONNAIRE, or SURVEY; however, THERE ARE MANY DIFFERENCES. Make sure you follow the specific examples.

---

issuing department/bureau/person's last name, first name. *title of document/questionnaire/survey* place of publication, publisher, issuing date. Series name, series no. [format].

NOTE: The information necessary for a document/questionnaire/survey citation can be found on the cover, on the title page, in a corner, and/or on the back of the item itself.

| Public document | Committee for Extension Education. *The Need for a Community College in Putnam County* Alta, ME: Marist College, December 1993 [public document]. |

| Government document | Communicable Disease Center. *Widget's Syndrome* Atlanta: U.S. Government Printing Office, 1992. Viral Disease Series, No. 15 [government document]. |

Organization document	Brewster Teachers' Association Welfare Fund. *The Welfunder*, Brewster, NY: Brewster Teachers' Association Welfare Fund, 1995 [newsletter].
Questionnaire	Archin Memorial Library. *What Public Library Services Have You Used?* n.p.: Archin Memorial Library, Summer 1989 [questionnaire].
Survey	Claus, Rudolph. *Additional Expenses Incurred During the Period Beginning November 25 and Ending December 25* Sleigh, NY: Rudolph Claus, February 17, 1992 [survey].

NOTE: Many times the issuing department/bureau/person is also the publisher; repeat the name if this is the case.

How Do You Write a Bibliographic Entry for the Congressional Record?

This is a general guide for a bibliographic entry for a *CONGRESSIONAL RECORD* reference. Make sure you follow the specific examples.

Congressional Record. date of legislative proceeding: page x.

NOTE: The information necessary for a *Congressional Record* reference can be found on the document itself.

Congressional Record	*Congressional Rec.* Aug. 16, 1994:7550–71.

How Do You Write a Bibliographic Entry for a Flyer, Poster, or Chart?

This is a general guide for a bibliographic entry for a FLYER, POSTER, or CHART. Be sure to follow the specific examples.

---

issuing organization/person's last name, first name. *title/subject of flyer/poster/chart.* place of publication: publisher, issuing date [format].

NOTE: The information necessary for a flyer, poster, or chart citation can usually be found on the back or in a corner of the item itself.

Flyer   Concerned Citizens of Mt. Morris. *School Consolidation: Yes or No.* n.p. Concerned Citizens of Mt. Morris, April 1989 [flyer].

NOTE: Sometimes the issuing organization/person is the same as the publisher; repeat the name if this is the case.

Poster   United Lobster Fishermen. *Ban Offshore Drilling.* Moosebay, ME: Moosebay Chamber of Commerce, 1990 [poster].

Chart   Dewey, Melvil. *The Dewey Decimal Classification.* Amherst: Media Charts, 1987 [chart].

How Do You Write a Bibliographic Entry for a Dissertation?

This is a general guide for a bibliographic entry for a DISSERTATION. Make sure you follow the specific examples.

---

author's last name, first name. "title of dissertation." place of publication/issuance: publisher/issuing agent, date of publication/issuance [format].

NOTE: The information necessary for a dissertation citation can be found on the document itself.

Published dissertation	McKiernan, Joseph A. "The Economic Impact of Computers on Secondary Social Studies Education." New City, NY: Social Trends Press, 1993 [published dissertation].
Unpublished dissertation	Lawrence-Russell, Julieanne. "Testing Procedures for Placement in Gifted and Talented Programs in Elementary Schools." Saratoga Springs, NY: St. Luther Univ., 1991 [unpublished dissertation].

How Do You Write a Bibliographic Entry for Correspondence?

This is a general guide for a bibliographic entry for CORRE-SPONDENCE. Make sure you follow the specific examples.

---

author's last name, first name. Identification of author. Correspondence to recipient's name. date of correspondence.

NOTE: The information necessary for a correspondence citation can be found on the document itself. Some of the information may not be available.

Personal correspondence	Dearborne, Henrietta. Correspondence to Erin Essex. March 20, 1994.
Business correspondence	Asp, James W. President of Tri-State Electronics. Correspondence to Paula Cox. May 17, 1993.
Open correspondence	Statz, Congressman Samuel S. Maine representative 23rd District. Correspondence to constituents. January 20, 1992.

How Do You Write a Bibliographic Entry for Unpublished Material?

This is a general guide for a bibliographic entry for UNPUB-
LISHED MATERIAL; however, THERE ARE MANY DIFFER-
ENCES. Follow the specific examples.
   Unpublished material is defined as printed matter that has
been released for *limited* distribution.

---

author's last name, first name. "title of unpublished material." place of issuance: issuing agent, date [unpublished
   material].

NOTE: The information necessary for an unpublished
        material citation can be found on the document
        itself. Some of the information may not be avail-
        able.

Information   Silver Spade Garden Club. "Spring
sheet   Gardening Guidelines." Silver Spade
                 Garden Club, 1990 [unpublished
                 material].

NOTE: Many times the author is also the issuing agent;
        repeat the name if this is the case.

Employee   Mohler, John Allan. "Some Issues of
notice   Concern." Bedford Heights, LA:
                 Board of Education, March 1993
                 [unpublished material].

Classroom   "Causes of the Revolutionary War."
handout   [unpublished material].

Church   Bargelo, Julia A., ed. "The Chimes."
bulletin   Weirton, WV: Sacred Heart on the
                 Hill, December 25, 1993
                 [unpublished material].

*How Do You Write a Bibliographic Entry for Material from
a Vertical File?*

This is a general guide for a bibliographic entry for VERTICAL
FILE MATERIAL; however, THERE ARE MANY DIFFERENCES.
Follow the specific examples.

If an item can be cited according to its particular category (magazine or newspaper article, pamphlet, etc.), use its appropriate
bibliographic documentation style. Sometimes the information
necessary for these items is incomplete or missing, in which case
the vertical file format should be used.

---

author's last name, first name. "title of specific item." place
of publication: publisher, date. [vertical file–format].

NOTE: The information necessary for a citation for ver-
        tical file material can usually be found on the
        item itself. Some of the information may not be
        available.

Map in   "Australia." Sydney, Austral.: Koala
vertical   Cartography, 1988. [vertical
file   file—map].

Documentation   "Marines Take Iwo Jima." New York:
missing   *New York Times*. [vertical file—
                newspaper article].

NOTE: In this case the author, date, and page number are
        missing.

*How Do You Write a Bibliographic Entry for
Secondary Source Material?*

This is a general guide for a bibliographic entry for SECONDARY
SOURCE MATERIAL; however, THERE ARE MANY DIFFER-
ENCES. Follow the specific examples.

If the secondary source material you are using is a book, use the basic form in the box. If it is not a book, use the specific bibliographic examples in this style guide.

Secondary source material is defined as a reference to part(s) of an original work/writing or to a segment(s) of firsthand research.

EXAMPLE:

A diary entry would be the original (primary) work, and a book quoting the diary would be the secondary source.

NOTE: When writing a bibliographic entry for a secondary source. ONLY the work actually used is cited.

---

author's last name, first name. *title of book.* place of publication: publisher, date of publication.

NOTE: The information necessary for a citation for secondary source material can usually be found on the title page, verso, table of contents page, box/container, introductory/concluding frames, in accompanying documentation, reference materials, media, and/or on the item itself.

Book containing book cited	Coyle, Harriet. *Human Nature in Hard Hard Economic Times.* Chicago: Univ. of Chicago Press, 1994.
Magazine containing book cited	Hesco, Nellie. "Famous Breeding Mares." *Horseman's Magazine.* July 1978.
Magazine containing newspaper article cited	Longworth, Mary Isabelle. "Politics and Values." *American Journal.* November 1991.

How Do You Write a Bibliographic Entry for an Adaptation?

This is a general guide for a bibliographic entry for an ADAPTA-TION; however, THERE ARE MANY DIFFERENCES. Follow the specific examples. Condensed/abridged works are written bibliographically in the same manner as adaptations. The following forms are for both PRINTED and NONPRINT materials.

---

adapter's last name, first name. "adapted title." Adaptation of "original title" [format] by author's name. place of publication of adapted work: publisher of adapted work, date of adaptation. [format].

NOTE: The information necessary for an adaptation citation can be found on the title page, verso, table of contents page, box/container, introductory/concluding frames, in reference materials, accompanying documentation, media, and/or on the item itself.

Short story adaptation of play

States, Sam. "The Red, White, and Blue." Adaptation of *Forever USA* [play] by Walter Nation. Philadelphia: Ben Franklin Press, 1986. [short story].

NOTE: *Forever USA* is underlined because plays are underlined; short works are in quotation marks.

Motion picture/video recording adaptation of book

Edsel, Betty. *Dynamite and Me.* Adaptation of *My Life With Peter* [book] by Mary Cohen. New York: Musical Theater Publications, 1954. [motion picture].

NOTE: *Dynamite and Me* is underlined because motion pictures are underlined.

Audio recording adaptation of poem

Flagg, Molly, composer. "Stand Up." Adaptation "Love of Country" [poem] by Nathan Hancock. Key Studio, 1990. [audiodisk JAM 321].

Filmstrip adaptation of motion picture/ video recording	"Sea Fight." Adaptation of *Country at War* [video recording]. Flynn Films, 1983. [filmstrip].
Printed speech adaptation of a nonprint speech	Roosevelt, Martha. "It's Time for a Woman." Adaptation of "It's Time for a Woman" [TV—NBC]. Political Printers, 1994. [print speech].
Condensed work	Hopeful, Faith. *A Midnight Ride.* Condensed version of *A Midnight Ride* [autobiography] by Charity W. Virtue. Juneau, AK: Platitude Press, 1985. [biography].
Abridged work	Brummel, Walter. *The Antique Lover's Abridged Guide.* Abridged version of *The Antique Lover's Guide* [book] by Cassie Eastlake. Tarrytown, DE: Beau Brothers, 1991. [book].

Entries for Nonprint Materials

How Do You Write a Bibliographic Entry for a Filmstrip?

This is a general guide for a bibliographic entry for a FILMSTRIP; however, THERE ARE MANY DIFFERENCES. Make sure you follow the specific examples. For ADAPTATIONS, see citations under Adaptation.

---

author's last name, first name. "title of filmstrip" producer/manufacturer, date of production/manufacture. [filmstrip].

NOTE: The information necessary for a filmstrip citation can usually be found on the introductory frames and/or on the box or container.

Single filmstrip with author	Hannibal, Caesar. "Historic Gaul." Alpine Pictures, 1987. [filmstrip].
Single filmstrip with no author	"Costuming With Sacks." Fifth Avenue Productions, 1989. [filmstrip].
Filmstrip with author, part of a set	Lord, Taylor. "Loveseat Couches." In *Interior Decorating*. Allan Ethan Manufacturing, 1992. [filmstrip].
Filmstrip with no author, part of a set	"Early American Coverlets." In *Bedroom Decorating*. May Altmann, 1990. [filmstrip].
Set of filmstrips with author	Faust, Colleen. *Office Procedures.* Beyer Maia Productions, 1993. [filmstrip].
Set of filmstrips with no author	*Nocturnal Animals.* Science Concepts, 1991. [filmstrip].

How Do You Write a Bibliographic Entry for a Media Kit?

This is a general guide for a bibliographic entry for a MEDIA KIT; however, you should follow the specific examples. For ADAPTATIONS, see citations under Adaptation.

A media kit is defined as two or more different nonprint media treated as one set, for example, a filmstrip and cassette.

---

author's last name, first name. *title of media kit.* producer/manufacturer, date of production/manufacturer. [format].

NOTE: The information necessary for a media kit citation
        can usually be found on the container, in accompa-
        nying documentation, and/or on the individual
        item itself.

Media Kit   Barr, C. *Candy Making*. Paul Peter's
with author   Productions, 1978. [2 filmstrips & 2
                       records].

Media Kit   *Salad Making*. Father Earth & Sons, 1992
with no author   [80 slides & cassette].

*How Do You Write a Bibliographic Entry for a Motion
Picture/Video Recording?*

This is a general guide for a bibliographic entry for a MOTION
PICTURE/VIDEO RECORDING; however, THERE ARE MANY
DIFFERENCES. Make sure you follow the specific examples. For
ADAPTATIONS, see citations under Adaptation.

   Motion pictures include feature-length films, single-reel films,
and film cartridges/loops; these can be 16 mm., 8 mm., and/or
super 8 mm.

   Video recordings include reel-to-reel videotapes, videocassettes, videodisks, and television.

---

title of item. producer/manufacturer, date of production/
   manufacture [format].

NOTE: The information necessary for a motion pic-
        ture/video recording citation can usually be found
        on the introductory/concluding frames, accompa-
        nying documentation, and/or on the box or con-
        tainer.

Feature-length   *Cameo of a Comedian*. Hollywood
motion picture   Productions, 1991 [feature-
                       length film].

Single-reel film	*Fun With Photography.* El Cine Releases, 1990 [single-reel film].
Film cartridge/loop	*The Comedic Fall.* Pratfall Releases, 1990 [film cartridge].
Reel-to-reel videotape	*Understanding the GNP.* Wall Street Publications, 1992. [videotape].
Video-cassette	*How to Use a Computer.* Easy Learn Manufacturing, 1994 [videocassette].
Videodisk	*Daffodil in the Meadow.* Fleur Creations, 1993 [videodisk].
Video recording, part of a series	*American Stocks in a Bear Market.* In *Economics for the Everyday Person.* Monetary Productions, 1989 [videocassette].
Television	*What Are We Going to Do With the Money?* August 8, 1992 [TV—ABC].

How Do You Write a Bibliographic Entry for an Audio Recording?

This is a general guide for a bibliographic entry for an AUDIO RECORDING; however, THERE ARE MANY DIFFERENCES. Make sure you follow the specific examples. For ADAPTA-TIONS, see citations under Adaptation.

Audio recordings include records, record albums, compact disks, audio cassettes, audio disks, and reel-to-reel audio tapes.

---

author's/composer's last name, first name, author/composer. *title of item.* performer's/artist's/narrator's/reader's/com-mentator's name, performer/artist/narrator/reader/com-mentator. producer manufacturer, date of production/manufacture [format identification number].

NOTE: The information necessary for an audio recording
        citation can usually be found on the box or con-
        tainer and/or on the item itself.

Single record with author and reader	Sirocco, Sonny, author. *Dust in the Wind Tales*. Connie Ellen Verbose, reader. Sweet Sounds, 1990 [audiodisk MU525].
Single record with no author/ composer	*Spring Raindrops*. Easy Records, 1992 [audiodisk NS417].
Single record with commentator and no author/ composer	*Weather and Energy: A Team*. Gayle Whyte, commentator. Mark Media, 1992 [audiodisk PC0788].
Record album with artist	*The Shakespearean Histories*. Sir Oliver Laurence, artist. Bacon Manufacturers, 1990 [album 941 VBG].
Single cassette with composer	Storm, T., composer. *An Avalanche of Love*. Mountain Melodies, 1994 [audiocassette PUL994].
Single cassette with composer and artist	Cumulus, Star B., composer. *Clouds in the Heavens*. Misty M. Martin, artist. Castover Productions, 1989 [audiocassette PUB86].
Single cassette with narrator and no author, part of a set	*Stories for a Rainy Evening*. Sonny Dusk, narrator. In *Nighttime Tales*. Weatherson, 1992 [audiocassette WTZ344].

Set of cassettes with author/ composer	Days, Stormy, author. *The Complete Collection of Weather Stories Throughout the World.* Wind Ridge Records, 1986 [3 audiocassettes HN546].
Set of cassettes with no author/composer	*Laboratory Safety.* Sims Labs, 1990 [5 audiocassettes ECOS12].
Reel-to-reel audio tape with no author/composer	*Sounds of Weather.* Scud Releases, 1991 [audiotape TDB986].
Compact disk with artist	*Candlelight Memories.* Julio Placido, artist. Wax Productions, 1994 [compact disk NAS517].

How Do You Write a Bibliographic Entry for Computer Software?

This is a general guide for a bibliographic entry for COMPUTER SOFTWARE; however, THERE ARE MANY DIFFERENCES. Make sure you follow the specific examples.

Computer software includes diskettes, tapes, disks, and CD-ROM.

"title of program." program writer's name. producer/manufacturer, date of production/manufacture [format].

NOTE: The information necessary for a computer software citation can usually be found on the introductory frames of the program, on the box or container, in the accompanying documentation, and/or on the item itself.

Diskette with program writer	"Word Derivatives." Nicholas W. Fig. Charles Hardson, 1993 [diskette].
Diskette with no program writer	"Vocabulary Study for the GRE." Lerose Com-u-ed, 1994 [diskette & manual].
Diskette with program writer, part of a set	"Compound Interest." Penelope O'Rourke. In *Business Math Problems*. Pascal Associates, 1993 [diskette & manual].
Tape with program writer	"The Inventory Master." Ronald Van Dyke. Count Creations, 1994 [computer tape].
Tape with no program writer	"Measuring As a Life Skill." Kirt Products, 1993 [computer tape].
Disk with program writer	"The Complete Library System." Dewey Archibald. Circulation Systems, 1992 [computer disk & manual].
Disk with no program writer	"The American Record Keeper." Data Enterprises, 1994 [computer disk & manual].
CD-ROM	"Authors of New England." Hawthorne/Emerson, 1994 [CD-ROM].

How Do You Write a Bibliographic Entry for a Microscope Slide?

This is a general guide for a bibliographic entry for a MICRO-SCOPE SLIDE; however, THERE ARE MANY DIFFERENCES. Make sure you follow the specific examples.

> "title/subject of the slide." producer/manufacturer, date of production/manufacture [microscope slide].

NOTE: The information necessary for a microscope slide citation can usually be found on the box or container and/or on the slide itself.

Single slide   "Paramecium." Barry Clement, 1986 [microscope slide].

Single slide,   "Seaweed Reproduction." In *Marine*
part of a set   *Organisms*. Fischer & Sons, 1991 [microscope slide].

Set of slides   *Fresh Water Protozoa*. O'Gorman Scientific Supply House, 1989 [microscope slide].

How Do You Write a Bibliographic Entry for a Photographic Slide?

This is a general guide for a bibliographic entry for a PHOTOGRAPHIC SLIDE; however, THERE ARE MANY DIFFERENCES. Make sure you follow the specific examples.

> photographer's last name, first name. "title/subject of the slide." producer/manufacturer, date of production/manufacture [photographic slide].

NOTE: The information necessary for a photographic slide citation can usually be found on the box or container and/or on the slide itself.

Single slide   Parsons, Patrick. "Friar Ambrose." Art
with   International, 1985 [photographic
photographer   slide].

| Single slide with no photographer | "Mob violence." Associated Press, 1989 [untitled photographic slide]. |

NOTE: When a photographic slide is untitled, describe it briefly, indicating any information that might be available on its origin.

| Single slide with photographer, part of a set | Gardener, Harold. "Daisy" In *Flowers of North America*. Botany, 1991 [photographic slide]. |

| Set of slides | *America's Cartoonists*. Appalachia Slides, 1989 [photographic slide]. |

How Do You Write a Bibliographic Entry for a Photograph?

This is a general guide for a bibliographic entry for a PHOTO-GRAPH; however, THERE ARE MANY DIFFERENCES. Make sure you follow the specific examples.

---

photographer's last name, first name. "title/subject of the photograph." producer, date of production. [photograph].

NOTE: The information necessary for a photograph citation can usually be found on the box or container and/or on the photograph itself.

| Single photograph with photographer | Trousseau, Felix. "The Wedding Ceremony." Oxford, 1987 [photograph]. |

| Single photograph with no photographer or title | "Abandoned child crying on railroad platform." n.d. [untitled photograph]. |

NOTE: When a photograph is untitled, describe it briefly, indicating any information that might be available on its origin.

Single photograph with photographer, part of a set

Daggeur, F.W. "Old woman with a bird." In *Aging*. Seniors Plus, 1990 [untitled photograph].

Set of photographs

Prince, Albert. *Clothing Styles of the Decade.* Ascot, 1991 [photograph].

How Do You Write a Bibliographic Entry for a Transparency?

This is a general guide for a bibliographic entry for a TRANS-PARENCY; however, THERE ARE MANY DIFFERENCES. Make sure you follow the specific examples.

---

producer's/manufacturer's last name, first name. "title/subject of the transparency." producer/manufacturer, date of production/manufacture [transparency].

NOTE: The information necessary for a transparency citation can usually be found on the box or container and/or on the transparency itself.

Single transparency with producer

Fulcy, Agatha. "Job Outlook in the Year 2010." Projections All, 1994 [transparency].

Single transparency with no creator or title

"Red color shades." Scarlet Tones, 1990 [untitled transparency].

NOTE: When a transparency is untitled, describe it briefly, indicating any information that might be available on its origin.

Single transparency with producer, part of a set	Zaka, Abu. "Somalia." In *Maps of the Dark Continent*. Abu Zaka, 1994 [transparency].
Set of transparencies	*Media References*. Instructional Services, 1994 [transparency].

How Do You Write a Bibliographic Entry for a Radio Broadcast?

This is a general guide for a bibliographic entry for a RADIO BROADCAST; however, THERE ARE MANY DIFFERENCES. Make sure you follow the specific examples. For ADAPTATIONS, see citations under Adaptation.

"title of individual broadcast." broadcaster's name, broadcaster. date of broadcast [radio—station/network].

NOTE: The information necessary for a radio broadcast citation can usually be found in the newspaper listings for the broadcast or taken from the broadcast itself.

Single broadcast	"The Abortion Amendment." Leo Boynton, broadcaster. November 2, 1994 [radio—KDKA].
Single broadcast, part of a series	"Interviews With the Candidates." Netty Kay Speaker, broadcaster. January 6, 1987. Part of *America Wants to Know* [radio—WABC].
Series of broadcasts	*Political Problems of the United Nations*. James R. Banner, broadcaster. May 14 to July 13, 1994 [radio—WNYC].

How Do You Write a Bibliographic Entry for a Piece of Realia?

This is a general guide for a bibliographic entry for a piece of REALIA; however, THERE ARE MANY DIFFERENCES. Make sure you follow the specific examples.

Realia is defined as a real or reproduced article used to enhance classroom instruction, for example, primitive tools, medieval costumes, rock specimens, or ancient coins.

---

title/subject of piece. producer/manufacturer/collector, date of production/manufacture/origin [realia].

NOTE: The information necessary for a realia citation can usually be found on the box or container. Some of the information may not be available.

Commercially produced realia	*Tools of the Aztecs.* Summerfall-Winterspring Productions, 1994 [realia].
Organization's collection of realia	*New York State Rocks.* New York State Geological Association Museum, 1991 [realia].
Individual's unlabeled collection of realia	*Commemorative stamps of U.S. Presidents.* Alfred F. Elhu, n.d. [unlabeled realia].

NOTE: If there is no information on the box or container, provide your own title.

How Do You Write a Bibliographic Entry for a Nonprint Speech, Lecture, or Sermon?

This is a general guide for a bibliographic entry for a nonprint SPEECH, LECTURE, or SERMON; however, THERE ARE MANY DIFFERENCES. Make sure you follow the specific examples. For ADAPTATIONS, see citations under Adaptation. The form below is for a NONPRINT speech, lecture, or sermon; for a

PRINTED speech, lecture, or sermon, see citations in the print section.

A nonprint speech, lecture, or sermon is defined as an oral message given before an audience for a specific purpose.

---

speaker's last name, first name. identification of speaker.
"title/subject of speech/lecture/sermon." location of
speech/lecture/sermon, date of speech/lecture/sermon.
[format].

NOTE: The information necessary for a nonprint speech,
        lecture, or sermon citation can usually be found in
        accompanying documentation or obtained at the
        time of the speech/lecture/sermon.

Classroom lecture	Balboa, Joseph. Professor of History. "American Explorations." Pioneer Univ., November 26, 1992 [classroom lecture].
Political speech	Harangue, Senator Paula. Chairwoman of Rules Committee. "Reelection." Civic Auditorium, October 30, 1993 [political speech].
Formal report	Conduit, Edward. Chairman of Citizens Water Treatment Committee. "Safe Water." Council Chambers, September 20, 1992 [formal report].
Commence-ment address	Patrick, Jennifer. Dean of Students at Gerrard College. "Keeping Up With the Joneses." Academy of Fashion & Design, August 17, 1993 [commencement address].
Sermon	Kierns, Ambrose, M.M. Maryknoll Missionary. "His Power." Bethany Church, March 22, 1993 [sermon].

NOTE: This form is used when the writer is *physically present* at the speech/lecture/sermon.

Speech on TV   James, David E. Political Analyst. "The 1984 Presidential Primary" Taken from *CBS Election Report* April 3, 1994 [TV—CBS].

Sermon on radio   Leopold, Judith A. Minister at Trinity Cathedral. "Baptism Gives New Life." Taken from *Sunday Morning Speaks*. February 29, 1996 [radio—WHUD].

How Do You Write a Bibliographic Entry for Nonprint Conference, Convention, or Seminar Proceedings?

This is a general guide for a bibliographic entry for a live or video CONFERENCE, CONVENTION, or SEMINAR. For the transcript of a conference, convention, or seminar, see citations in the print section.

A nonprint conference, convention, or seminar is defined as the live or video proceedings of a conference, convention, or seminar.

> sponsoring organization's name. "title of conference/convention/seminar." location of conference/convention/seminar, date of conference/convention/seminar [format].

NOTE: The information necessary for the live or video proceedings of a conference, convention/seminar can usually be found in accompanying documentation or at the time of the conference/convention/seminar.

Live conference/ convention/ seminar proceedings   "Health Benefits International. "Controlling Prices." London, October 1994 [conference].

Video conference/ convention/ seminar proceedings	"Murphy Fire Installations. "New Fire Codes." Yonkers, NY, February 1995. [video seminar].

How Do You Write a Bibliographic Entry for a Distance Learning Presentation?

This is a general guide for a bibliographic entry for a DISTANCE LEARNING presentation.

"title of individual presentation." name of course. name of presenter, identification of presenter. date of transmission, transmission location [distance learning—format].

NOTE: The information for a distance learning presentation can usually be found in accompanying documentation or obtained at the time of the presentation.

Distance learning via television	"Habitats of Gorillas." Advanced Biology. Stacey Hodge, teacher. March 21, 1995. Brewster, NY [distance learning—TV].
Distance learning via radio	Australia's Early Inhabitants—Aborigines. Australian History. Melba Simpson, lecturer. Sept. 1, 1996. Alice Springs, Austr. [distance learning—radio].

How Do You Write a Bibliographic Entry for a Nonprint Interview?

This is a general guide for a bibliographic entry for a nonprint INTERVIEW; however, THERE ARE MANY DIFFERENCES. Make sure you follow the specific examples. The form below is for a NONPRINT interview; for a PRINTED interview see citations in the printed materials section.

---

interviewee's last name, first name. identification of interviewee. Interviewed by interviewer's name. "subject/title of interview." location of interview, date of interview.

NOTE: The information necessary for a nonprint interview citation can usually be obtained at the time of the interview.

Personal
interview
   King, Jerome. Sportscaster. Interviewed by Julianna F. Kimberly. "College Recruitment." Memorial Stadium, January 6, 1992.

NOTE: This form is used when the writer is *physically present*, i.e., conducting the interview or observing it firsthand.

Interview
on TV
   Miceli, Mikel Jon. Italian Ambassador. Interviewed by Patsy Fosina. "Italian-American Economic Relationship." Taken from *Meet the Press*. October 2, 1994 [TV—CBS].

Interview
on radio
   Harrison, Josephine. Career Consultant. Interviewed by Kelliann Roberts. "Networking." Taken from *Weekend Job Market*. April 11, 1993 [radio—WPUT].

NOTE: If an interview is untitled, provide your own title based on the subject.

How Do You Write a Bibliographic Entry for a Microform?

This is a general guide for a bibliographic entry for a MICROFORM; however, THERE ARE MANY DIFFERENCES. Make sure you follow the specific examples.

Microform includes microfilm and microfiche.

---

author's last name, first name. *title of microfilm/microfiche.*
  producer/manufacturer, date of production/manufac-
  ture [format identification number].

NOTE: The information necessary for a microform citation
        can usually be found on the container and/or on
        the item itself. Not all microforms have identifica-
        tion numbers.

Microfilm with author	Fleischhauer, Sigmund, M.D. *The Effects of Microwaves on the Unborn.* Microfilms of Canada, 1989 [microfilm 35-1625].
Microfiche with no author	*Report of the President's Commission on Curriculum Development in Health.* Univ. of Colorado, 1990 [microfiche ERIC Document ED 525 137].
Microfiche with no author, part of a set	*Genealogical Records of the Timoney Family.* In *Families of Ireland.* Longford, Ireland: Univ. of Donegal, 1990 [microfiche 6 27 56].

How Do You Write a Bibliographic Entry for Creative Arts?

This is a general guide for a bibliographic entry for the CRE-
ATIVE ARTS; however, THERE ARE MANY DIFFERENCES.
Make sure you follow the specific examples. For a type of artistic
work not given here, use the basic form in the box.

Creative arts include sculpture, paintings, blueprints, musical
compositions, etc.

---

creator's last name, first name. *title/subject of work.* date
  [format].

NOTE: The information necessary for a creative arts citation can usually be found in the accompanying
documentation or on the item itself.

Sculpture	Vincenzo, Luigi. *Mother and Child*. 1894 [sculpture].
Painting	Roger, C. Jolly. *Sailing the Blue Horizon*. 1839 [painting].
Blueprint	Moody, Blaise. *Fine Arts Hall of New Mexico*. 1985 [blueprint].
Musical composition	Firman, Wilhelmina. *Mein Deutschland*. 1942 [musical composition].
Single musical work	Debs, Nelson. "The March of the Green Bears." 1980 [musical composition].
Single work as part of a longer musical composition	Mars, April. "Jumping Jupiter." 1968. In *The Heavenly Planets Serenade* [musical composition].

*How Do You Write a Bibliographic Entry for a Telephone Call or
Conference Call?*

This is a general guide for a bibliographic entry for a TELE-
PHONE/CONFERENCE CALL.

last name of person(s) called, first name. Identification of
person(s) called. Called by caller's name. "subject of tele-
phone/conference call." date of telephone/conference

NOTE: The information necessary for a telephone/con-
ference call citation can be obtained at the time
of the call.

Telephone   Kilcommons, Peter. Business Manager of
call   North United School District. Called
                        by Mary Northrup. "Employee
                        Assistance Program." May 15, 1993.

Conference call   Board of Trustees. Brewster Teachers'
                        Welfare Fund. Called by John
                        Fischer. "Benefit Updates." June 19,
                        1994.

Electronic Resources

What Is an Electronic Resource?

An electronic resource may include the Internet*, World Wide Web*, electronic mail (e-mail)*, electronic bulletin boards*, online databases*, etc.

Do Electronic Resources Present Special Citing Problems?

Yes, the rapidly increasing sources of electronic media—Internet, E-mail, World Wide Web, online databases, etc.—have created serious problems for researchers, teachers, librarians, writers, and students.

One of the major difficulties is the changing nature of information. If you have the title, author, publisher, date of publication, etc. of a book, it is usually fairly simple to locate the source of the citation. However, electronic sources cited today may be altered, moved, or deleted tomorrow.

Citation elements that have always been considered essential parts of a citation such as page numbers, date of publication, or publisher may not be available for electronic sources.

Additional information such as *date accessed* may need to be included in the citation for an electronic source since information can be changed frequently.

Path information containing punctuation which may be confused with punctuation found in traditional citation forms may require new ways of dealing with this problem.

*These terms are defined in the glossary.

107

While the Uniform Resource Locator (URL)* may become the
preferred method for finding Internet information, at the present
time several different ways of accessing the same information
contributes to the problems faced by individuals trying to
develop efficient and adequate citation models.

It is clear that researchers need standardized forms for citing
electronic sources. Individuals who have developed their own
citation forms and made them available through electronic
sources have been deluged with requests for copies of their work
from teachers, students, librarians, writers, etc.

Such standardized citation forms are not available at the present
time (Spring, 1997) despite the fact that national and international
organizations have been attempting for several years to agree on
such a form. The rapidly expanding and changing nature of these
electronic sources along with increased experience with earlier, and
inadequate, citation models adds to the problems faced by organizations and individuals trying to provide satisfactory citation forms.

Obviously, despite these difficulties and delays, researchers
must have some method of citing electronic sources *now* since
increasing numbers of individuals are using these resources for
research purposes.

Are There General Guidelines for Citing Electronic Resources?

Yes, in addition to using the models below for citing electronic
sources, certain general guidelines need to be considered.

1. Check with your instructor to determine if a specific style
   guide for citing electronic sources is required and available.
2. If no specific electronic-sources style sheet is recommended
   or required, use these general guidelines for citing these
   sources. *Keep in mind the basic reason for citing a source is to
   permit the retrieval of the information cited.* Because of the
   complex nature of electronic sources and the many difficulties previously mentioned, a fundamental rule should be
   that the *information must be as complete as possible.*
3. A useful check to see if your citation will lead the reader to
   your source could involve reviewing the data and steps you
   have listed to determine if an interested individual following your citation information could successful access your
   source if such information were still available at that site.

4. Another method of handling the problem of retrieving information from electronic sources might involve printing out a copy of material to be cited and including it with your research paper. This does not, of course, replace a citation of the material, but this step could be useful for material which might be altered or deleted before the citation can be verified or examined.

5. Because constant changes are being made to some forms of electronic material it is important that the date you *accessed* the material becomes part of your citation. The *date of publication/creation/updating/revision* should also be included as part of the citation.

6. Information for the citation can usually be taken directly from the electronic source, but additional information is sometimes available on accompanying documentation, packaging, disk, or from the librarian, etc.

7. Because of the complex nature of finding information via electronic sources, citations will probably be much longer than citations for print media. However, it is important to include *all* of the necessary information to retrieve the citation without regard to the length of the data. MORE IS BETTER!

8. When citing an electronic source include the edition/version if provided.

9. Pointed brackets (⟨ ⟩) are being used to enclose some electronic addresses,such as URLs, which prevents confusion with other punctuation which may be used in the citation. A slash (/) may be used to separate elements when listing a reference path.

10. Since extra and missing spaces, errors in punctuation or in upper/lower case letters can cause problems with retrieval, extreme care should be taken to cite the electronic address/pathway precisely.

11. Unlike citations for more traditional sources, those for electronic resources list the publication and access dates on a *day*/month/year sequence. Example: 17 April 1997.

12. If using the APA style, the publication/creation date follows the author.

13. To clarify an electronic address/path, words such as via, available, linked from (Lkd.), published in, or accompanied by (for listing documentation) may be useful. If it is absolutely impossible to determine the source being used, a

general term such as electronic or electronic source may be used.

14. Despite the differences between citing electronic resources and more traditional media such as books and magazines, certain conventions, abbreviations, etc. remain the same. For instance, institutions/organizations may be listed as author, the title may be the first element in a citation when no author is given, titles for complete works should be underlined or italicized, titles of single works or sections/parts of a larger work should be enclosed in quotation marks, the abbreviation n.d. is used for no date, the abbreviation n.p. (no place, no publisher, no page) is usually used in electronic source citations to indicate no page, editors, translators, or compilers should be identified using the proper abbreviations. Use conventions and abbreviations established for traditional media sources If they do not conflict with the guidelines or citation models for electronic sources.

Are There Current Citation Trends for Electronic Resources?

Yes, while no standards for the citing of electronic sources have been established, certain trends and solutions to citing problems have emerged. The guidelines and the following citation forms are based on these trends and solutions in an effort to provide a common sense approach to a complex and evolving situation. Keep in mind the general guidelines above; and most important, provide as much information as possible to guide the reader to the source of your citation. Good luck.

How Do You Write a Footnote Entry for an Electronic Resource?

This is a general guide for footnoting an ELECTRONIC RESOURCE. Please note all of the guidelines above.

---

author's name. "title." *title of full work,* if applicable. Publisher/ producer, if available creation/updating/revision date. <URL> /electronic address/menu path (access date).

How Do You Write a Bibliographic Entry for an Electronic Resource?

This is a general guide for a bibliographic entry for an ELEC-TRONIC RESOURCE. Please note all of the guidelines above.

---

author's last name, first name. "title." *title of full work,* if applicable. publisher/producer, if available date of publication/creation/updating/revision. <URL>/electronic address/menu path (access date).

Checklists

Before using the following checklists, go back and verify the research/term paper assignment to see that

_____ the topic has been adhered to;

_____ the proper number of sources and/or citations has been used;

_____ the required style, format, and documentation have been followed;

_____ and the length of the assignment has been met.

When these steps have been completed, the work is ready to be checked. This is often difficult, but it is an extremely important task. For this reason four checklists are included here.

BEFORE TYPING FINAL DRAFT

1. Content—to check for clarity of ideas
2. Grammar—to check the mechanics of expression
3. Format—to check the rules of proper documentation

AFTER COMPLETION OF FINAL DRAFT

4. Proofreading—to check for typographical errors

Content Checklist

_____ The purpose of the paper is set forth at the outset and developed throughout the paper.

_____ The title is creative and appropriate for the subject.

_____ The topic is developed clearly and logically.

_____ The beginning paragraph(s) of the text capture(s) the reader's interest.

_____ The paper maintains the reader's interest throughout.

_____ The outline has been followed.

_____ All material relates to the subject.

_____ Information is not repeated unnecessarily.

_____ Each paragraph develops its topic sentence.

_____ Each paragraph is developed coherently.

_____ Clear transitions link paragraphs throughout the paper.

_____ Where necessary, material is footnoted properly.

_____ Ending paragraph(s) provide(s) an effective conclusion.

Grammar Checklist

_____ The outline follows parallel structure.

_____ Each sentence expresses a complete thought; fragments and run-on sentences have been avoided.

_____ A variety of sentence types and lengths are used.

_____ Sentence beginnings are varied.

_____ Sentences are punctuated properly.

_____ Capital letters are used correctly.

_____ Cliches, trite expressions, and other overworked terms generally have been avoided.

_____ Formal/informal language is used carefully.

_____ Vocabulary is varied and appropriate.

_____ Modifiers are interesting and colorful.

_____ Verb tenses and moods are correct.

_____ Subjects and verbs agree.

_____ All pronoun references are clear.

_____ Transitional devices are used carefully and appropriately.

_____ There are no usage errors.

_____ Words are spelled correctly.

_____ When necessary, words are hyphenated properly.

_____ Words/terms are abbreviated correctly.

Format Checklist

_____ All quotations are noted properly.

_____ Quotations of four or more lines are indented correctly.

_____ Any references to other parts of the paper are clear.

_____ All footnote/note and bibliographic information is accurate.

_____ The form of all footnote/note and bibliographic citations is correct.

_____ Either traditional or modern footnote/note notation is used consistently.

_____ If shortened terms are used, they appear in both footnote/note and bibliographic citations.

_____ The standard bibliography includes all sources mentioned in the footnotes/notes.

_____ Footnote/note numbers in the text are consecutive and placed properly.

_____ All footnote/note citations are numbered consecutively.

_____ Bibliographic citations are not numbered.

_____ Half title pages, if used, precede all sections after the text.

_____ If applicable, computer concerns have been addressed.

Proofreading Checklist
(after printing final draft)

_____ Title page has complete information.

_____ Correct margins have been maintained.

_____ Proper spacing has been used.

_____ Quotations of four or more lines have been indented appropriately.

_____ Paragraphs have been indented uniformly.

_____ All footnote/note and bibliographic citations have been indented correctly and consistently.

_____ The parts/sections of the paper have been headed properly and are in correct order.

_____ All footnote/note citations have been numbered consecutively.

_____ Bibliographic citations have not been numbered.

_____ Pages have been numbered correctly.

_____ There are no spelling or other typographical errors.

_____ All corrections have been made neatly and carefully.

_____ A copy of the entire paper has been made.

Word Processing

Before typing a research/term paper, you must complete the following steps:

_____ finalize your outline;

_____ write your final draft;

_____ assemble your footnotes; and

_____ alphabetize your bibliography entries.

When you have completed these steps, you are ready to type your paper.

General Guidelines

Typing paper is generally the standard 8 1/2 by 11 inches. Paper for ordinary use should be of good quality. For an advanced type of assignment, a special grade of paper may be required.

Your instructor may prefer a particular method of making corrections. ALWAYS MAKE YOUR CORRECTIONS NEATLY AND CAREFULLY.

A margin of at least one inch should be maintained on each side of the text. If you intend to put your paper into a folder, allow an extra half-inch on the inside margin.

Unless otherwise specified, the text of your paper should be double spaced. The preliminary pages of a paper use single spacing, however, and footnote and bibliography entries are always single spaced.

The general rule for underlining is to use a continuous line; however, with computers often it is not possible to underline the spaces between words. Foreign words or expressions that are not commonly accepted as part of the English language should also be underlined or italicized.

When a number can be expressed in one or two words, spell it out (for example, ninety or twenty-two). In most other cases, use numerals. Compound words and fractions use a hypen. Never begin a sentence with a numeral; always spell the number out or revise your sentence. Of course, numerals are always used for a date, phone number, address, time, page number, or decimal and with abbreviations such as in., 1., pp., or mm.

Refer to a standard handbook for grammatical questions such as capitalization, punctuation, and outline headings and subheadings.

A full research term paper uses two methods of pagination. Although counted, the title and half title pages are not numbered; all other pages are numbered. All pages *preceding* the first page of text are consecutively numbered using lower-case Roman numerals (see glossary) at the bottom of each page.

The first page of text is page one and can be left unnumbered or numbered at the bottom center. The second page of text and all succeeding pages should be numbered consecutively using Arabic numerals. Page numbers can be placed in the upper right-hand corner, centered at the top of the page, or centered at the bottom of the page.

It is extremely important that you proofread carefully the final copy before submitting it. Use the checklists included here.

If you plan to type your paper on a computer, there are certain issues that must be addressed. First, ask your instructor if a computer copy will be acceptable. Then, give thought to the type of paper and printer available.

Consider your needs and the limitations of the word processing program you will use. Certain programs do not provide for such functions as subscripts, superscripts, or solid underlining.

Since many factors can cause the loss of your work, be safe and always make a backup.

ALWAYS make a copy of your final paper before submitting it. If it's typewritten, make a carbon copy; if it's computer printed, run a second copy. In either case, *at least* make a photocopy.

THESE RECOMMENDATIONS MAY CONFLICT WITH LOCAL PRACTICES OR REQUIREMENTS, SO IT IS WISE TO CHECK WITH YOUR INSTRUCTOR WHO MAY HAVE RULES THAT DIFFER.

Arrangement of Parts of Paper

Now you are ready to arrange the parts of your paper for typing. The usual order of a paper is:

1. title page
+2. contents/table of contents
+3. preface*/foreword*/introduction*
+4. acknowledgments*
+5. outline
+6. list of tables
+7. list of illustrations
+8. abstract*
9. text
10. footnotes/notes/endnotes*
11. bibliography/sources cited/works cited*
+12. supplementary bibliography/sources consulted*
+13. appendix*
+14. chronology*
+15. glossary*
+16. index*

+optional parts and/or for advanced papers only

Explanation of Parts of Paper

TITLE PAGE

The title page usually includes the title of the paper, the writer's name, the course name and/or number, the instructor's name, and the date submitted. This information is arranged on the page in various formats. See sample pages in the Appendix.

*These terms are defined in the glossary.

The title page is the first page of the paper.

CONTENTS/TABLE OF CONTENTS
(usually for advanced papers only)

The table of contents, also known as the contents, is a listing of the chapters/sections or other formal divisions of a paper. Its purpose is to give an overview of the material included and the order of presentation. It is optional to include the preliminaries such as the preface, introduction, or acknowledgments; however, the table of contents itself is never included.

The term "contents" or "table of contents" is capitalized, centered, and about two inches from the top of the page. The first line of type begins on the third line below this head. See the table of contents at the beginning of this style guide.

The table of contents would follow the title page.

PREFACE/INTRODUCTION
(usually for advanced papers only)

The preface, also known as the foreword, is an *informal* statement whose purpose is to introduce the material to the reader.

The introduction is the *formal* preliminary guide to the paper which makes a brief statement of the scope, aim, and general character of the research/topic.

The term "preface" or "introduction" is capitalized, centered, and about two inches from the top of the page. The first line of type begins on the third line below these heads.

The preface/foreword/introduction would be the next page of the paper.

ACKNOWLEDGMENTS
(usually for advanced papers only)

The acknowledgment is a simple statement in which the writer recognizes the person(s) or institution(s) to whom he or she is grateful for *special, nonroutine* assistance.

The term "acknowledgments" is capitalized, centered, and about two inches from the top of the page. The first line of type begins on the third line below this head.

Acknowledgments would be the next page of the paper.

OUTLINE
(optional)

An outline provides a framework for the ideas developed in the text and can be put into sentence or topic form.

Instead of the term "outline," the title of your paper is capitalized, centered, and about two inches from the top of the paper. The first line of type begins on the third line below the title. See sample pages in the Appendix.

If used, the outline would be the next page of this paper.

LIST OF TABLES
(usually for advanced papers only)

A table is a columnar arrangement of statistics. The list of tables, also known as tables, consists of the captions/titles of all tables in the text and their page numbers.

The term "tables" or "list of tables" is capitalized, centered, and about two inches from the top of the page. The first line of type begins on the third line below this head. See sample pages in the Appendix.

The list of tables would be the next page in the paper.

LIST OF ILLUSTRATIONS
(usually for advanced papers only)

Illustrations can be photographs, diagrams, maps, graphs, or any other material that explains or clarifies the text in a graphic or pictorial fashion. The list of illustrations consists of the captions/titles of all illustrations in the text and their page numbers.

The term "illustrations" or "list of illustrations" is capitalized, centered, and about two inches from the top of the page. The first line of type begins on the third line below this head. See sample pages in the Appendix.

The list of illustrations would be the next page in the paper.

ABSTRACT
(usually for advanced papers only)

An abstract is a succinct summary of the ideas in a paper. If required, follow the format, placement, etc., specified by your instructor.

TEXT

The text is the main body of your paper in which your data/explanations/findings are presented. Regardless of its length, your paper should include introductory information, full development of your topic, and a summary/conclusion.

Advanced papers may be divided into chapters/sections; if very long, subtitles/subsections may be necessary for organization and clarification. A typical progression of three levels for subtitles/subsections might be:

1. heading—centered and in capital letters
2. sideheading—flush left and in upper and lower case letters
3. heading at beginning of paragraph—indented and underlined or italicized

EXAMPLE:

RELIGION OF THE AMERICAN INDIAN

Iroquois Nation

Prior to the coming of the white man. Early inhabitants of the forests

Paragraphs should be indented five to eight spaces. Choose whichever is comfortable, but be consistent.

If you included in the text a quotation that will be more than three typewritten lines, omit the quotation marks, indent the quotation about one-half inch from the right- and left-hand margins, and single space the quotation. Quotes of three lines or less are incorporated into the text and set off by quotation marks. In both situations the footnote number goes at the *end* of the material being quoted. See sample pages in the Appendix.

An ellipsis, i.e., three spaced dots (...), is used to show an omission of a word or words. It is used whether the omission occurs at the beginning, at the end, or within the text of the quote. Should the omission follow a punctuation mark, the ellipsis is used after the mark. The ellipsis (at the beginning or the end of the quote) is included *within* the quotation marks, if they are used.

If your typewriter does not have brackets ([ ]), carefully insert them by hand using ink to match the color of your ribbon.

FOOTNOTES/ENDNOTES

Footnote entries can be placed at the *bottom* of the page(s) containing their corresponding footnote numbers or at the *end* of the research/term paper in a separate section. When these entries are at the bottom of the page, they are called footnotes. When they appear at the end of a paper, they are often called endnotes, with the page titled "notes."

When notes are typed on a separate page, the term "notes" is capitalized, centered, and about two inches from the top of the page. The first line of type begins on the third line below this head.

If you can choose where to put footnotes, you will find it easier to type them in a separate section.

The footnote/note number is placed before the entry. The first word is indented from five to eight spaces with the number before the word; the second and subsequent lines are out to the margin. All footnote/note entries are single spaced, with a double space between entries.

For more detailed information on the use of the footnote, see specific footnote questions at the beginning of the book. For examples of footnote/note entries, see sample pages in the Appendix.

If notes are placed at the end of the research/term paper, the note section follows the text.

BIBLIOGRAPHY/SOURCES CITED/
REFERENCES/WORKS CITED

The standard bibliography—also known as sources cited, references, or works cited—is the final listing of the materials actually cited in a paper. This section provides the complete information necessary for a reader who wishes to locate the materials cited in the footnotes/notes.

An entry begins with the author's last name and starts at the margin. Second and subsequent lines are indented the same number of spaces as the first line of a footnote/note.

All entries are listed in alphabetical order according to the author's last name, or the first word of the title if there is no author. (Should the title begin with "A," "An," or "The," alphabetize according to the second word.)

If more than one book by the same author is listed, in the second and subsequent entries his or her name may be replaced by a straight line approximately ten characters in length.

The term "bibliography," "sources cited," "references," or "works cited" is capitalized, centered, and about two inches from the top of the page. The first line of type begins on the third line below this head. See sample pages in the Appendix.

The bibliography may either precede or follow the appendix.

SUPPLEMENTARY BIBLIOGRAPHY
(optional)

The supplementary bibliography, also known as sources consulted, is a listing of the materials used but not actually cited in a paper.

Entries are made in the same manner as for a bibliography.

The term "supplementary bibliography" or "sources consulted" is capitalized, centered, and about two inches from the top of the page. The first line of type begins on the third line below this head. See sample pages in the Appendix.

The supplementary bibliography begins on a separate page and immediately follows the bibliography.

APPENDIX
(optional)

The appendix is a section containing supplementary material that the writer does not want to include in the text but feels is important for the reader to have.

The term "appendix" is capitalized and centered on a half title page preceding the appendix section. See the Appendix page of this style guide.

The appendix may either precede or follow the bibliography.

CHRONOLOGY
(optional)

The chronology is a list that gives the exact dates of events arranged in the order in which they occurred.

The term "chronology" is capitalized, centered, and about two inches from the top of the page. The first line of type begins on the third line below this head. See sample pages in the Appendix.

The chronology may be either a part of the appendix or a separate section that can be put in multiple positions at the end of the paper.

HALF TITLE PAGE
(usually for advanced papers only)

The half title page is a page containing only the title of the section it precedes, for example, the appendix, glossary, or index. It is usually used only for sections following the text. If you use a half title page for one section, be consistent and use it for all.

The title of the section is capitalized, centered on the line, and halfway down the page. See half title pages before Appendix, Glossary, and Index sections of this style guide.

GLOSSARY
(optional)

The glossary is an alphabetical listing of selected words or terms related to the topic of the paper. It is usually found at the back of a work.

The term "glossary" is capitalized, centered, and about two inches from the top of the page. The first line of type begins on the third line below this head. See Glossary at the end of this style guide.

In a paper the glossary never precedes the footnote section, but it can be in multiple positions at the end of the paper.

INDEX
(optional and for advanced papers only)

The index is an alphabetical listing indicating on what pages to find topics, names, etc.

The term "index" is capitalized, centered, and about two inches from the top of the page. The first line of type begins on the third line below this head. See Index at the end of this style guide.

The index is always the last section of a paper.

Appendix

Appendix A: Underlining/Quotation Marks/Italics

As a general rule, the title of a short work, single piece, or part of a long work is in quotation marks. The title of a longer work, series, or set is placed in italics (if available) or underlined. Following is a brief chart for quick reference.

U	=	underlined
Q	=	quotation marks
I	=	italics
N	=	none of these

Title/subject of work	U	Q	I	N
almanac	x		x	
atlas	x		x	
audio recording				
set	x		x	
single	x		x	
Bible				x
blueprint	x		x	
book	x		x	
bulletin		x		
CD-ROM		x		
chart	x		x	
computer software				
set	x		x	
single		x		
conference				
individual session		x		
title	x		x	

Title/subject of work	U	Q	I	N
conference call		x		
Congressional Record	x		x	
convention				
individual session		x		
title	x		x	
correspondence				x
creative arts				
long work	x		x	
part of long work		x		
single work	x		x	
dictionary	x		x	
dissertation		x		
distance learning		x		
ditto		x		
document	x		x	
encyclopedia				
article		x		
volume/set	x		x	
essay		x		
filmstrip				
set	x		x	
single		x		
flyer	x		x	
information sheet		x		
interview				
nonprint		x		
printed		x		
lecture		x		
map		x		
media kit	x		x	
microform				
set	x		x	
single	x		x	
microscope slide				
set	x		x	
single		x		
motion picture	x		x	
musical work				
long composition	x		x	
single		x		
opera	x		x	
painting	x		x	

Title/subject of work	U	Q	I	N
pamphlet	x		x	
periodical				
article		x		
column		x		
editorial		x		
magazine	x		x	
newspaper	x		x	
review		x		
photograph				
set	x		x	
single		x		
photographic slide				
set	x		x	
single		x		
play	x		x	
poem				
long, published as book	x		x	
single		x		
poster	x		x	
questionnaire	x		x	
radio broadcast				
series	x		x	
single		x		
realia	x		x	
sculpture	x		x	
seminar				
individual session		x		
title	x		x	
sermon		x		
short story		x		
speech		x		
survey	x		x	
telephone call		x		
television program	x		x	
transparency				
set	x		x	
single		x		
unpublished material		x		
video recording				
series	x		x	
single	x		x	

Appendix B:
Abbreviations

Here are some abbreviations you may encounter in doing your research/term paper.

Abbreviation	Meaning	Example/Notes
abr.	abridged, abridgement	
abs.	abstract	
A.D.	in the year of the Lord	A.D. 775 (no space between letters; comes before year)
adapt.	adapted by, adaptation	
a.k.a.	also known as	preface, a.k.a. foreword
anon.	anonymous	(not used in foot-notes or biblio-graphy entries when author unknown; list under title)
app.	appendix	
art., arts	article(s)	
assn.	association	
assoc.	associate, associated, association	
b.	born	b. 1942
B.C.	before Christ	775 B.C. (no space between letters; comes after year)
B.C.E	before Christian era	775 B.C.E. (same as B.C., without Christian bias)

Abbreviation	Meaning	Example/Notes
bib. biblio., bibliog.	bibliography	
biog.	biography, biographer, biographical	
bk., bks.	book(s)	
bull.	bulletin	
c, ©	copyright	c 1983, © 1983
c., ca.	about	c. 1994, ca. 1994
cf.	compare, compare with	cf. Four Freedoms (compare with Four Freedoms)
ch., chs. chap., chaps.	chapter(s)	
chor.	choreographer, choreographed by	Lindsay Brown, chor.
cit.	citation, cited	
col., cols.	column(s)	
comp.	compiler, compiled by	J. McLaughlin, comp.
cond.	conductor, conducted by	Gregory Miles, cond.
cont.	continue, continued	
d.	died	d. 1988
dir.	director, directed by	Mary Koerner, dir.
diss.	dissertation	
DOS	Disk Operating System	(computer term)
ed., eds.	editor(s), edited, edition	Joseph Mack, ed. ed. by Edward Leo 3rd ed.
e.g.	for example	e.g., nuclear bomb (no spaces; set off by commas)
esp.	especially	11. 24–9, esp. 1. 25
et al.	and others	Nia Ashbridge, et al. (used mostly with works having three or more authors)
f., ff.	following page(s)	pp. 19f., pp. 19ff.
fax, facs., facsim.	facsimile	
fig., figs.	figure(s)	

Abbreviation	*Meaning*	*Example/Notes*
fn., fns.	footnote(s)	
fwd.	foreword, foreword by	
GPO	Government Printing Office	
ibid.	in the same place	(refer to Traditional Notation section)
id.	the same as previously mentioned	
i.e.	that is	i.e., Bach (no spaces; set off by commas)
il., ill., illus.	illustration(s)	
inc.	incorporated, including, included, inclusive	
incl.	including, inclusive	
inst.	institute, institution	
intl.	international	
intro.	introduction	
jour.	journal	
l., ll.	line(s)	1. 34, 11. 34–40
LC	Library of Congress	
legis.	legislation, legislator, legislative, legislature	
loc. cit.	in the place cited	(refer to Traditional Notation section)
ltd.	limited	McKiernan, Ltd.
misc.	miscellaneous	
ms., ms, mss.	manuscript(s)	
n., nn.	note(s)	
narr.	narrator, narrated by	Nan Thomas, narr. narr. Sid North
n.b., N.B.	note well	N.B. the enclosed map
n.d.	no date	(usually used to mean publication date is unknown)
no., nos.	number(s)	
n.p.	no place no publisher no page	(place of publica- tion/publisher/page number is not known)
op. cit.	in the work cited	(refer to Traditional Notation section)

Abbreviation	Meaning	Example/Notes
orch.	orchestrated, orchestra	orch. by Ashley Tate
p., pp.	page(s)	p. 51, pp. 51–6
par., pars.	paragraph(s)	p. 24, par. 2
passim	here and there	pp. 505–15 *passim*
per se	by itself, of itself	loyalty per se
perf.	performed, performer	perf. D'arcy Clair
pl.	plural	
pl., pls.	plate(s)	pl. IV, pls. IV and X
pref.	preface	
prod.	producer, produced	Darryl Simpson, prod.
pseud.	pseudonym	Mark Twain, pseud. (for Samuel Clemens)
pt., pts.	part(s)	
pub.	published, publication, publisher	pub. 1989, 1989 pub.
q.v.	which see	
RAM	random access memory	(computer term)
repr.	reprint, reprinted by	
rev.	review, reviewed, revised, revision	rev. of *Latin Poetry* rev. by Ambrose Jose rev. ed.
ROM	read-only memory	(computer term)
sc.	scene	sc. viii
sec., secs.	section(s)	
ser.	series	
sess.	session	
[sic]	thus	(used when quoting material containing an error or startling information; always in brackets [sic])
st., sts.	stanza(s)	
supp.	supplement	
tr., trans.	translator, translation, translated	Edward Leo, tr., Latin trans., trans. by Edward Leo
v., vs.	versus, against	Brewster v. Harrison Brown vs. Board of Education

Abbreviation	Meaning	Example/Notes
VCR	videocassette recorder, videocassette recording	
viz.	namely	viz., Abe Lincoln
vol., vols.	volume(s)	
vs., vss.	verses(s)	vs. 4, vss. 4–8

State and Territory Abbreviations

Alabama	AL
Alaska	AK
American Samoa	AS
Arizona	AZ
Arkansas	AR
California	CA
Canal Zone	CZ
Colorado	CO
Connecticut	CT
Delaware	DE
District of Columbia	DC
Florida	FL
Georgia	GA
Guam	GU
Hawaii	HI
Idaho	ID
Illinois	IL
Indiana	IN
Iowa	IA
Kansas	KS
Kentucky	KY
Louisiana	LA
Maine	ME
Maryland	MD

Massachusetts	MA
Michigan	MI
Minnesota	MN
Mississippi	MS
Missouri	MO
Montana	MT
Nebraska	NE
Nevada	NV
New Hampshire	NH
New Jersey	NJ
New Mexico	NM
New York	NY
North Carolina	NC
North Dakota	ND
Northern Mariana Is.	MP
Ohio	OH
Oklahoma	OK
Oregon	OR
Pennsylvania	PA
Puerto Rico	PR
Rhode Island	RI
South Carolina	SC
South Dakota	SD
Tennessee	TN
Texas	TX
Trust Territories	TT
Utah	UT
Vermont	VT
Virgin Islands	VI
Virginia	VA
Washington	WA
West Virginia	WV
Wisconsin	WI
Wyoming	WY

Country Abbreviations

Australia	Austral.
Austria	Aus.
Belgium	Belg.
Canada	Can.
Denmark	Den.
England	Eng.
France	Fr.
Great Britain	Gt. Brit.
Greece	Gr.
Ireland	Ire.
Israel	Isr.
Italy	It.
Japan	Jap.
Netherlands	Neth.
New Zealand	NZ
Portugal	Port.
Scotland	Scot.
Spain	Sp.
Sweden	Swed.
Switzerland	Switz.
Union of Soviet Socialist Republics (former)	USSR
United Kingdom	UK

Appendix C: Sample Pages

Title Page

The following title pages are general guides. Ask your instructor about the specific information required.

THE POLITICAL PEREGRINATION

OF

JOHN DOS PASSOS

_____

A Paper

Presented to

Dr. George Wise

Eastern Ridge State College

_____

In Partial Fulfillment

of the Requirements

for

English 562

_____

by

Nancy E. Abrams

June 1997

LASERS: FRIEND OR FOE?

Shaun O. McCarthy
July 31, 1997

Outline

The following pages show a topic outline and a sentence outline.

HENRIK IBSEN, PLAYWRIGHT

I. Personal life

II. Literary style

III. Contemporaries

   A. influence of
   B. influence on

IV. Scope of his writings

V. Analysis of selected plays

   A. *A Doll's House*
      1. synopsis
      2. character development
      3. author's motivation

   B. *Ghosts*
      1. synopsis
      2. character development
      3. author's motivation

   C. *An Enemy of the People*
      1. synopsis
      2. character development
      3. author's motivation

   D. *Hedda Gabler*
      1. synopsis
      2. character development
      3. author's motivation

VI. Comparison of female characters in selected plays

VII. Reaction to Ibsen's works

   A. contemporary times
   B. present times

VIII. Chronology

V–J DAY

Six years after the German invasion of Poland, the Japanese signed the "Instrument of Surrender" ending the Second World War.

I. Many events in World War II were directly related to V–J Day.

II. The Potsdam Conference commenced on July 17, 1945.

    A. The members of the Conference conferred in Cecilienhof.

    B. Two of the three representatives were fairly new.

    C. The main topics discussed were of national importance.
        1. The surrender of Japan was the main point of concentration.
        2. The decision to use the atom bomb was a weighty one.

    D. The Potsdam Declaration was the greatest result of the Conference.
        1. Russia did not sign the Declaration.
        2. The Declaration did not consider three important points.
            a. The payment of reparations was overlooked.
            b. International exchange went unconsidered.
            c. Tariffs were also left out.
        3. The Declaration allowed for the release of imprisoned persons.

    E. The Japanese looked upon the Declaration with conflicting views.

III. The use of the atom bomb was finally decided.

IV. Following the disaster, Japan was unsure of its position.

List of Tables

Tables are numbered consecutively throughout the paper. Note the placement of table numbers and page numbers in the following sample.

LIST OF TABLES

List of Illustrations

Illustrations are numbered consecutively throughout the paper. Note the placement of figure numbers and page numbers in the following sample.

LIST OF ILLUSTRATIONS

Figure   Page

Chart

Don't forget to title each chart, whether on a separate page within the text or incorporated on a page of the text.

Presidential Elections, 1824–1860

Year	Candidates	Popular Vote	Electoral Vote
1824	John Quincy Adams	108,740	84
	Andrew Jackson	153,544	99
	Henry Clay	47,136	37
	William H. Crawford	46,618	41
1828	Andrew Jackson	647,231	178
	John Quincy Adams	509,097	83
1832	Andrew Jackson	687,502	219
	Henry Clay	530,189	49
	others	33,108	18
1836	Martin Van Buren	761,549	170
	Wm. Henry Harrison	549,567	73
	Hugh L. White	145,396	26
	Daniel Webster	41,287	14
1840	Wm. Henry Harrison	1,275,017	234
	Martin Van Buren	1,128,702	60
1844	James K. Polk	1,337,243	170
	Henry Clay	1,299,068	105
	James G. Birney	62,300	0
1848	Zachary Taylor	1,360,101	163
	Lewis Cass	1,220,544	127
	Martin Van Buren	291,263	0
1852	Franklin Pierce	1,601,474	254
	Winfield Scott	1,386,578	42
1856	James Buchanan	1,838,169	174
	John C. Fremont	1,335,264	114
	Millard Fillmore	874,534	8
1860	Abraham Lincoln	1,865,593	180
	Stephen A. Douglas	1,382,713	12
	John C. Breckinridge	848,356	72
	John Bell	592,906	39

Notes

The following pages show:

    A. traditional notation, with footnotes at bottom

    B. modern notation, with notes at end

It is permissible to use either the modern or traditional notation at the bottom of each page or on a separate page(s) at the end of the text. Check with your instructor to ascertain which form of notation and footnote/note placement is preferred. Be consistent throughout your paper.

Footnotes

information. Students must "learn how to learn."[2]

Under the pressure of this mandate and with the pro-
liferation of new types of audiovisual equipment, software, and reference materials, the media specialist had
begun to experiment with new teaching methods in order
to find a solution to the problem of trying to teach too
much to too many students.

An additional and related need for this type of study
involved what Hug termed "technological responsibility"
and which he defined as a "cost-effective, process-product
. . . approach to the solution of educational problems."[3] In
such difficult economic times, school systems were under
great pressure from taxpayers to effect economies.

Along with this demand for economy, the word
"accountability" had been heard with increasing
frequency. It may be pertinent to consider at this
time the position taken on this subject by some
of the most powerful and effective organizations in

2. Ibid.
3. William E. Hug, *Instructional Design and the Media Program*
(Chicago: American Library Association, 1975), pp. 2–3.

Endnotes

As one writer pointed out, "if we wish to state concisely the difference between Sunni and Shī'a we should say that the former is a church founded on the consent of the community, the latter is the authoritarian church."[6]

To make some analogy to Christianity we might compare the Sunni-Shī'a schism to the Protestant-Roman Catholic split.

The Sunni feel that individuals can stand directly before God without intermediaries, while Shī'a see the imam as the intercessor with Allah. The Sunni have a more flexible approach recognizing the possibility of alternative acceptable systems of *shari'a* from which the faithful could choose within broad limits,[7] and contrary to one author's statement,[8] the Sunni should be considered the "Protestants" of the Islamic world.

On the other hand, the Shī'a developed a philosophy which could be compared to the Roman Catholic idea of papal infallability since Shī'a believe that Muslims should accept authoritative teaching, doctrine of ta'lim, as espoused by the imam. The imam is viewed by the Shī'a as a divinely appointed leader with superhuman qualities

Notes

1. Desmond Stewart, *Early Islam* (New York: Time, 1967), p. 59.

2. Joseph Schacht, *The Legacy of Islam* (Oxford: Clarendon Press, 1974), p. 160.

3. H. A. R. Gibb and J. H. Kramers, *Shorter Encyclopedia of Islam* (Leiden, Netherlands: E. J. Brill, 1961), p. 634.

4. John L. Esposito, *Islam and Development: Religion and Sociopolitical Change* (Syracuse: Syracuse Univ. Press, 1980), p. 52.

5. Marshall G. S. Hodgson, *The Order of the Assassins* (Gravenhage, Netherlands: Mouton and Company, 1955), p. 8.

6. Alfred Guillaume, *Islam* (New York: Penguin Books, 1954), p. 120.

7. Hodgson, p. 6.

8. Michael Curtis, *Religion and Politics in the Middle East* (Boulder, CO: Westview Press, 1981), p. 364.

9. Guillaume, p. 117.

10. Bernard Lewis, *Islam and the Arab World* (New York: Alfred A. Knopf, 1976), p. 37.

11. Guillaume, p. 119.

12. Michael M. J. Fisher, *Iran: From Religious Dispute to Revolution* (Cambridge, MA: Harvard Univ. Press, 1980), p. 10.

Bibliography

The following pages show

A. a standard bibliography

B. a supplementary bibliography

C. a bibliography using the APA style

D. an annotated bibliography

BIBLIOGRAPHY

Amrine, Michael. *The Great Decision.* New York: G.P. Putnam's Sons, 1959.

Benns, F. Lee. *European History Since 1870.* New York: Appleton-Century-Crofts, 1955.

————. *Europe Since 1914.* New York: Appleton-Century-Crofts, 1957.

Butow, Robert J.C. *Japan's Decision to Surrender.* Stanford: Stanford Univ. Press, 1954.

Flower, Desmond and James Rieves. *The Taste of Courage, The War, 1939–1945.* New York: Harper & Brothers, 1960.

Greenfield, Kent Roberts, ed. *Command Decisions.* New York: Harcourt, Brace, 1959.

Henschel, Robert and Clark Lee. *Douglas MacArthur.* New York: Henry Holt, 1952.

Hunt, Frazier. *The Untold Story of Douglas MacArthur.* New York: Devin-Adair Company, 1954.

Kovacs, Arpad F. *The Twentieth Century.* New York: St. John's Univ. Press, 1961.

Muzzey, David Saville. *Our Country's History.* Boston: Ginn, 1957.

Togo, Shigenori. *The Cause of Japan.* Tr. and ed. by Fumihiko Togo and Ben Bruce Blakeney. New York: Simon & Schuster, 1956.

Whitney, Courtney. *MacArthur, His Rendezvous with History.* New York: Alfred A. Knopf, 1956.

SUPPLEMENTARY BIBLIOGRAPHY

Ausubd, Nathan. *Voices of History, 1945–46.* New York: Gramercy Publishing Co., 1946.

Bruun, Geoffrey. *The World in the Twentieth Century.* Boston: D.C. Heath, 1957.

Eichelberger, Robert L. *Our Jungle Road to Tokyo.* New York: The Viking Press, 1950.

Fuller, J.C.F. *A Military History of the Western World.* New York: Funk & Wagnalls, 1956.

Gunther, John. *The Riddle of MacArthur, Japan, Korea and the Far East.* New York: Harper & Brothers, 1951.

Wildes, Harry Emerson. *Typhoon in Tokyo.* New York: Macmillan, 1954.

BIBLIOGRAPHY

Brown, J. D., Collins, R. L., and Schmidt, G. W. (1988). Self-Esteem and Direct Versus Indirect Forms of Self-Enhancement. *Journal of Personality and Social Psychology.* 55 445–453.

Brown, R. (1989). Testing and Thoughtfulness. *Educational Leadership.* 46 (7) 31–33.

Children at Risk: The Work of the States. (1987). Washington, DC: Council of State School Officers.

Clemes, H. and Bean, R. (1981). *Self-Esteem: The Key to Your Child's Well Being.* New York: Kensington.

Donnelly, M. (1987). *At-Risk Students.* (ERIC Digest Series Number 21). Eugene, OR: ERIC Clearinghouse on Educational Management.

Ekstrom, R.B., Goertz, M.E., Pollack, J.M., and Rock, D.A. (1986). Who Drops Out of High School and Why? Findings From a National Study. *Teacher's College Record.* 87 (3) 356–373.

Hargreaves, K. (1993). Classroom Assessment Techniques. Lectures given during IRI Learning Center course. Yorktown Heights, NY.

Holly, W.J. (1987). Self-Esteem: Does It Contribute to Students' Academic Success? Eugene, OR: University of Oregon, Oregon School Study Council.

Manchur, C. (1990). But . . . the Curriculum. *Phi Delta Kappan.* 71 (8) 634–637.

ANNOTATED BIBLIOGRAPHY

Bolin, Luis. *Spain: The Vital Years*. Philadelphia: J.B. Lippincott, 1967.

As part of the intrigue which brought Francisco Franco to the leadership of the Nationalists, the author gives a detailed account of the events immediately before and after the Spanish Civil War.

Carr, Raymond. *Spain 1808–1939*. London: Oxford Univ. Press, 1966.

A survey of the economic, social, and political origins of modern Spain as well as an examination of the factors which militated against political stability.

Gibson, Ian. *The Death of Lorca*. Chicago: J. Philip O'Hara, 1973.

Details not only the death of Garcia Lorca but the years and events in Granada which created the atmosphere for what has been called one of the great crimes of the Spanish Civil War.

McKendrick, Melveena. *Horizon Concise History of Spain*. New York: American Heritage Publishing, 1972.

A part of the Horizon series on countries of the world and provides a well illustrated and readable history of Spain from Paleolithic times to the era after the Spanish Civil War.

Payne, Stanley G. *Franco's Spain*. New York: Thomas Y. Crowell, 1967.

A short biography of Franco which establishes the background to understand the long dictatorship which Spain experienced. The effects of the Falange, army, church, and *Opus Dei* as well as Spain's position during World War II are covered.

Chronology

Note that the date controls the divisions of a chronology.

CHRONOLOGY OF SOME HENRIK IBSEN WORKS

1849 – *Cataline*—first verse drama; written under pseudonym Brynjolf Bjarme

1853 – *St. John's Night*—first play he wrote for the National Theatre; a failure

1856 – *The Feast at Solhaug*—first success

1857 – *The Vikings in Helgeland*—attempted to free himself of contemporary Danish influence

Olaf Liljekrans

1858 – Director of the Norwegian Theatre

1864 – *The Pretenders*—first important play

1867 – *Peer Gynt*

1869 – *The League of Youth*—first political play

1873 – *Emperor and Galilean*—last poetic play; Ibsen's favorite

1877 – *Pillars of Society*—first real dramatic success

Most popular modern dramatist in Germany

1879 – *A Doll's House*—won victory for himself and for realism in the theatre

1881 – *Ghosts*

1882 – *An Enemy of the People*

1888 – *Hedda Gabler*—play best designed for theatrical representation

1892 – *The Master Builder*—last great play

1899 – *When We Dead Awaken*

Glossary

Glossary

abridge   To create a shortened version of an original work. Abridgment sometimes involves a change of format. To cite an abridged version of a work, follow the footnoting and bibliographic style given for adaptations.

abstract   A succinct summary of the ideas in a paper.

acknowledgments   A simple statement in which the writer recognizes person(s) or institution(s) to whom he or she is grateful for special assistance.

acronym   A word formed from the first letters of the words in a phrase, e.g., UNICEF (United Nations International Children's Emergency Fund).

adaptation   A shortened or modified form of a literary work.

addendum (pl. addenda)   Information added to a book or document

American Psychological Association   An organization that publishes a style manual used by researchers, especially in the anthropological and psychological sciences.

ampersand   A symbol (&) meaning "and."

annotated bibliography   See **bibliography, annotated**

anonymous   Name unknown.

anthology   A collection of selected writings by one or various authors.

APA. See **American Psychological Association**

appendix (pl. appendices; appendixes)   Supplementary material that the writer does not want to include in the text but feels is important for the reader to have.

article   A short written piece on a specific subject.

audio recording   A disk or tape upon which sound has been inscribed.

audiocassette   A cartridge containing tape for recording sound.

audiodisk   A recording of sound on a flat, round surface.

audiotape   A magnetic strip for recording sound.

bibliography, annotated   Explanatory or critical notes/comments on a listing of works.

167

bibliography, preliminary   An initial listing of sources, compiled prior to starting formal research, to determine if enough material is available on a subject.

bibliography, standard   The final listing of the materials actually cited in a paper. Also called sources cited, works cited, or references.

bibliography, supplementary   A listing of the materials used but not actually cited in a paper, also called sources consulted. This is an optional listing.

bibliography, working   A listing of materials used while gathering information and writing a paper.

boldface   A thick, heavy type font, used for emphasis.

brackets   A pair of marks ([ ]) used to enclose words, figures, or symbols; also called square brackets.

business correspondence. See **correspondence, business**

caption   A title or heading of a page, article, chapter, etc., or under a picture explaining it.

caret   A mark (^) to show where something should be inserted.

cassette. See **audiocassette; videocassette**

CD. See **compact disk**

CD-ROM   A compact disk on which a large amount of digitalized read-only data can be stored.

chart   An exhibit of information in tabular, graphic, or other form.

chronology   A list of events arranged in the order in which they occurred.

citation   A footnote or bibliographic reference to a source of information.

cite   To quote from a printed or nonprint work.

column   A regularly featured article found in a periodical. It is usually signed and presents the writer's views.

commentator   A person who makes explanatory or critical observations, usually through some form of nonprint media.

common knowledge   Knowledge that is general, ordinary, and widespread.

compact disk   A small disk used to record sounds that are read by a laser beam.

compiler   A person who selects materials from various sources and puts them into a single work, usually a collection/anthology.

computer software   A program for a computer system; diskettes, tapes, and disks used for computers.

computer tape   A magnetic strip for recording computer programs.

condense   To create a shortened version of an original work. Condensing sometimes involves a change of format. To cite a condensed version of a work, follow the footnoting and bibliographic style given for adaptations.

conductor   A director of an orchestra, chorus, etc.

conference   A meeting of interested persons to discuss a specific subject.

conference call   A meeting via telephone of two or more individuals to discuss a specific subject.

Congressional Record   A printed transcript of the proceedings of the U.S. Congress.

convention   A meeting of interested persons to discuss a specific subject.

copyright date   The date a work was registered and protected by law.

correspondence, business   A formal communication by letter, usually of a professional or commercial nature.

correspondence, open   A communication by letter on a subject relating to the interests of a specific group, e.g., a legislator to his or her constituents.

correspondence, personal   An informal communication by letter, usually of a private nature.

creative arts   Original works of the imagination, e.g., painting, blueprints, musical compositions, sculpture, dance.

cross reference   A direction to the reader to go to another part of a work, e.g., See photography; See also HIV.

digest   A condensation, abridgement, or summary of a work.

director   A person who plans and supervises the performance of a stage, radio, television, or motion picture production.

disk   A type of computer software used to store information.

diskette   A piece of computer software; floppy disk.

dissertation   A formal paper written by a doctoral candidate.

distance learning   A method of education or training employing telecommunications to transmit information to a distant target.

document, government   A legal or official paper issued by a governing agency or institution.

document, organization   An official paper issued by an organization to its members or subscribers.

document, public   An official paper issued by a nongovernmental agency.

documentary   An artistic or dramatic presentation of factual information in a motion picture or video recording.

documentation   Explanatory information accompanying various forms of nonprint material.

DOS   An acronym for Disk Operating System.

draft, final   The completed, totally revised version of a paper from which the copy to be submitted is typed.

draft, preliminary   The early, "brainstorming" stage of writing, before the scope or direction of research has been determined.

draft, working   The rough copy used while writing a paper. Usually there are multiple working drafts, each with specific revisions.

dramatization   Arrangement into the form of a play.

editorial   A written or spoken statement expressed in mass media which reflects the opinion of the writer or speaker.

electronic bulletin board (ebb)   A computer system which acts as a message and information service for it users.

ellipsis   Three spaced dots (. . .) showing an omission of a word or words in a quotation.

E-mail   Messages or documents sent or received from personal computers using a special computer code.

endnotes   Footnotes listed in a separate section at the end of a paper.

entry   A statement or term entered or recorded in a book, list, etc.

ERIC   The Educational Resources Information Center. ERIC is a part of the government network that collects, stores, and distributes information pertaining to education.

errata (pl. of erratum)   A listing of printing errors and their corrections inserted in a book.

essay   A short literary piece written on a specific subject.

fax   A copy (facsimile) of printed matter transmitted electronically.

feature-length film   A full-length motion picture.

fictionalization   An imaginative or fictional version of actual events.

file transfer protocol (ftp)   A computer term for the procedure which permits the transfer of files from one computer to another.

film cartridge. See **film loop**

film loop   A short motion picture whose ends are spliced together to form a continuous length of silent or sound film.

final draft. See **draft, final**

floppy disk   A piece of computer software; diskette.

flyer   A notice, announcement, advertisement, etc., usually printed on one page and distributed by hand.

font   A specific size and style of type.

footnotes   Acknowledgments of the source of material, comments on material, or explanatory notes about material.

foreword. See **preface**

format   The design, plan, style, or organization of printed or nonprint material.

frame   An individual unit of a film, videotape, or computer program.

glossary   An alphabetical listing of selected words or terms related to a topic.

government document. See **document, government**

Government Printing Office   Official printing agency of the U.S. government.

half title page   A page of a paper containing *only* the title of the section it precedes.

ibid.   Used in traditional footnote notation for consecutive references to the same source. See discussion of traditional notation in the footnote section.

interactive media   Forms of communication that permit an individual to respond, e.g., a videodisk player linked to a computer.

interactive video   A two-way system of electronic communication, e.g., video recording and computer.

Internet   An electronic network that enables subscribers to access vast and varied databases and to communicate with other subscribers via personal computers.

interview   An information-gathering conversation between two or more individuals for broadcast or publication. An interview may be in printed or nonprint form.

introduction   A brief, formal preliminary statement of the aim, scope, and general character of a work.

ISBN   An acronym for international standard book number, the number assigned to a book at the time of publication for international identification.

issuing date   The date material is made available for public distribution.

issuing department/bureau   The agency responsible for the creation and release of material printed for public distribution.

italic   A sloping type font, used for emphasis.

justify   To space the words and letters in a line of type so that full lines have even margins on the left and right.

kit. See **media kit**

laser disk   A disk imprinted with digital information such as music, pictures, or text which is read or replayed by a laser beam.

lecture   An oral (nonprint) or written (printed) message presented to an audience for a specific purpose.

Library of Congress Classification System   Combinations of letters and numbers used to classify books and other materials. This classification system is used by many larger libraries instead of the Dewey decimal system.

loc. cit.   Used in traditional footnote notation for nonconsecutive references to the same source which refer to the same page number(s). See discussion of traditional notation in footnote section.

lower case   Printed in noncapitalized letters.

media, nonprint   Forms of communication, such as radio, television, and motion pictures, which reach large numbers of people.

media, printed   Forms of communication, such as books, newspapers, and magazines, which reach large numbers of people.

media kit   Two or more different nonprint media treated as one set.

microfiche. See **microform**

microfilm. See **microform**

microform   A photographic reproduction reduced in size, such as microfilm or microfiche. Microforms can be enlarged to readable size by magnifying viewers.

microscope slide. See **slide, microscope**

monograph   A book or article, especially a scholarly one, about a particular subject.

narrator   One who in speech or writing tells or recounts a story, event, or experience and/or provides additional information.

newsletter   An organization's letter or report presenting information to its members or subscribers, usually on a periodic basis.

nonprint media. See **media, nonprint**

notes   The term used as a heading for endnote listings. See also **endnotes; footnotes**

novelization   Arrangement in the form of a novel.

NTIS   The National Technical Information Service, part of a national clearinghouse established by the government to collect, store, and distribute scientific, technical, and engineering information.

online database   A large amount of material organized for convenient use via computer.

op. cit.   Used in traditional footnote notation for nonconsecutive references to the same source which refer to different page numbers. See discussion of traditional notation in footnote section.

open correspondence. See **correspondence, open**

optical disk. See **laser disk**

orchestrated   Composed or arranged for performance by an orchestra.

outline, final   The completed framework of the ideas developed in a paper.

outline, preliminary   The beginning framework of the ideas to be developed in a paper.

outline, sentence   A final outline in which all headings and subheadings are written in full sentences.

outline, topic   A final outline in which all headings and subheadings are written in words or phrases using parallel structure.

outline, working   The changing framework of the ideas being developed in a paper.

pagination   The system of numbering pages in a written work.

pamphlet   A short soft-cover booklet.

paraphrase   A restatement of another's ideas in different words.

parentheses   A set of curved lines ( ) used to set off information.

path A computer term used to indicate the route taken to retrieve or locate a file.

periodical A publication issued at regular intervals, e.g., magazines, newspapers.

personal correspondence. See **correspondence, personal**

photographic slide. See **slide, photographic**

plagiarism The failure to acknowledge the source of material and/or the claiming of someone else's words or ideas as one's own.

poster A large printed sheet or notice put up in a public place.

precis A summary or abstract of a written work.

preface (also foreword) An informal statement introducing the subject to the reader.

preliminary bibliography. See **bibliography, preliminary**

preliminary draft. See **draft, preliminary**

primary source. See **source, primary**

printed media. See **media, printed**

producer The person responsible for presenting an artistic work.

program writer One who creates a computer program.

proofreading The reading of a written work to mark errors to be corrected and/or material to be changed.

pseudonym An author's pen name.

public document. See **document, public**

questionnaire A written list of questions used to gather information, obtain a sampling of opinion, etc.

RAM Random-access memory (a computer term).

realia Actual or reproduced articles used to enhance classroom instruction, e.g., rock collections, coins, costumes.

reel to reel The process by which videotape or audiotape is transferred from one open reel to another.

reference Direction to a source of information.

references. See **bibliography, standard**

release date The date on which material is available to the public.

reprint Reproduction of a printed work without alterations.

research paper A systematic investigation, inquiry, or search for facts, principles, etc., organized into a written, fully documented paper.

review A written or spoken discussion/evaluation of a book, play, movie, TV program, etc., giving its merits and/or faults.

revision An amended or altered version of a work.

ROM Read-only memory (a computer term).

Roman numerals A system of notation used in pagination and outlining. Examples of the Roman numeral system:
I = 1; II = 2; III = 3; IV = 4; V = 5; VI = 6; VII = 7; VIII = 8; IX = 9; X = 10; L = 50; C = 100; D = 500; M = 1,000.

secondary source. See **source, secondary**

section   A division of a printed or written work.

seminar   A meeting of a group of people engaged in discussion and research under the guidance of an authority or expert.

sentence outline. See **outline, sentence**

series   A number of related printed or nonprint items arranged in a specific sequence.

sermon   An oral (nonprint) or written (printed) message presented to an audience for a specific purpose, usually religious.

shilling mark. See **slash**

sic   Used when quoting material containing erroneous or startling information; always put in brackets [sic].

single-reel film   A short motion picture.

slash   A mark (/) used in printed material between two or more words to indicate that whichever is appropriate may be used.

slide, microscope   A small, thin piece of glass on which an object is placed in order to examine it under a microscope.

slide, photographic   A small transparent photograph made of film or glass.

sound recording. See **audio recording**

source, primary   Original work/writing or firsthand research, e.g., diaries, manuscripts, records.

source, secondary   Reference to part of an original work/writing or to a segment(s) of firsthand research.

sources cited. See **bibliography, standard**

sources consulted. See **bibliography, supplementary**

speech   An oral (nonprint) or written (printed) message presented to an audience for a specific purpose.

spine   The part of a book which connects the front and back covers and usually shows the author and title.

standard bibliography. See **bibliography, standard**

stanza   A group of lines of a poem or song, usually four or more, arranged according to a fixed plan.

style guide   An aid to proper style, format, and documentation in a term/research paper. Also called style manual or style sheet.

subheading   A title or heading of a subdivision of text.

subscript   A letter, number, or symbol written slightly below a line, e.g., H_2O.

subtitle   A secondary title of a book, article, etc.

superscript   A letter, number, or symbol written slightly above a line, e.g., 4^3.

supplementary bibliography. See **bibliography, supplementary**

survey   A formal or informal study, examination, or poll to determine opinions, conditions, etc.

symposium   A meeting or conference at which several speakers discuss or present a topic.

synopsis   A brief statement or a summary giving a general view of some subject.

tape. See **audiotape; computer tape; videotape**

term paper   An inquiry, investigation, or search for knowledge, or an expression of opinion, organized into a written paper.

thesis   A formal paper by a candidate for a diploma or degree.

title page   A page at the beginning of printed material which contains bibliographic information; the first page of a research/term paper.

topic outline. See **outline, topic**

transcript   A printed copy or reproduction of material; the written record of live proceedings.

translator   One who converts printed or nonprint material from one language to another.

transparency   A piece of clear material on which an image has been produced for visual projection.

unpublished material   Material that has not been reproduced for sale or mass distribution.

upper case   Printed in capital letters.

verse   A short division of a chapter in the Bible; a stanza of poetry or song.

verso   The reverse side of the title page.

vertical file   A library's collection of charts, pamphlets, circulars, bulletins, newspaper clippings, etc., about topics of interest.

videocassette   A cartridge containing tape for recording images and sounds.

videoconference   A meeting of people at distant locations, made possible by the use of television sets, microphones, and special telephone equipment.

videodisk   A recording of images and sounds on a flat, round disk.

video recording   A tape or disk upon which images and sounds have been inscribed.

videotape   A magnetic strip for recording images and sounds.

virgule. See **slash**

working bibliography. See **bibliography, working**

working draft. See **draft, working**

working outline. See **outline, working**

works cited. See **bibliography, standard**

World Wide Web   A part of the Internet which provides graphics, audio, and video as well as text.

yearbook   A book published annually, containing information, statistics, pictures, etc.

Index

Index

electronic bulletin board (ebb),
    107
electronic resources:
    bibliography for, 111
    definition of, 107
    footnote for, 110
ellipses (. . .), 123
E-mail, 107
encyclopedias:
    bibliography for, 68–69
    footnote for, 24
endnotes. *See* notes
entries. *See* specific items, e.g.,
    books; magazines;
    filmstrips, etc.
ERIC, 59, 103–04
essays:
    bibliography for, 75–76
    footnote for, 31–32

feature length films. *See* motion
    pictures/video recordings
figures. *See* list of illustrations
film cartridges/loops. *See*
    motion pictures/video
    recordings
films. *See* motion
    pictures/video recordings
filmstrips:
    bibliography for, 88–89
    footnote for, 44–45
flyers:
    bibliography for, 81–82
    footnote for, 37–38
footnotes:
    abbreviated form of, 16–19
    abbreviations in, 17–19
    additional information in,
        10–11
    comments in, 10–11

definitions in, 11
direct quote in, 9–10
entries. *See* specific items,
    e.g., books; plays;
    filmstrips, etc.
explanatory statement in, 11
ibid in, 14
information needed for;
    nonprint media, 6–7
    print media, 4–6
loc. cit. in, 14–15
modern notation in;
    samples of, 15–16, 20
    use of, 15, 153, 155–56
numbering of, 12–13
op. cit. in, 14–15
paraphrases in, 9–10, 13
placement of, 20–21, 119, 123
purpose of, 9–12
reference in, 11–12
samples of, 14–16, 19–20,
    153–54
second and subsequent
    references in, 14–16
secondary source materials
    in, 20
shortened terms in, 16–19
spacing of, 13
traditional notation for;
    samples of, 14–15, 19,
        153–54
    use of, 14–15
types of, 9
See also notes
foreward. *See* preface
format checklist, 115

glossaries, 125, 167–75
government documents. *See*
    documents

About the Authors

Nancy E. Shields (B.A., Marymount College; M.L.S., Long Island University; M.S. Connecticut State University; C.A.S., State University of New York–Albany) has twenty-one years' experience as a library media specialist in private and public high schools in New York. In addition to administering high school libraries, she has taught research and media skills. As an adjunct to graduate degree work in the United States, she has done research in England and studied libraries and educational institutions in several foreign countries. She is the author of two other reference books.

Mary E. Uhle holds a B.A. in English from St. John's University and an M.S. in curriculum and instruction from Siena Heights College, Michigan. She is currently teaching English and developmental writing at Brewster High School in New York.